**What they're sayir**

Dr. Amanda "Tammy" Goodson is a true testament of being a tried and tested leader. This book is will take you on an awesome journey of accountability, spirituality, and leadership. *Astronomical Leadership* illustrates how to navigate through failures to generate more success and not compartmentalize who you are through your personal, spiritual, and professional journey. You will enjoy this introspective read because it illuminates limitless possibilities to create far-reaching personal/leadership opportunities and outcomes.

DR. WAYNE RICHARDS JR.
Strategic Systems Engineering Services (SSES)
Program Manager, Raytheon
Huntsville, AL

In *Astronomical Leadership*, Dr. Amanda H. Goodson presents a recipe for success with her Input, Process, Output program along with her Goodson 9 Block offering wisdom and insight in all nine areas of life: Finances, Relationships, Energy, Spirituality, Health, Work, Innovation, Leisure, and Long Life. This is a must read for anyone looking for a step-by-step way to reawaken your passions and have a clearer vision for the life you want to lead!

OLIVER "BO" LESLIE
National Chair, The Career Communications Group
St. Louis, MO

Dr. Goodson is a woman of great accomplishments who embodies strong and ethical leadership. Having known Amanda for many years professionally and personally, one example of her leadership tenacity stands out. I recall as part of a University Outreach event, we were asked to speak to audiences ranging from advanced or university-level to elementary school children. When visiting the elementary schools, Dr. Goodson employed a simple yet profound analogy to convey complex life lessons, explaining that she was going to teach them, "How to drive a CAR!" She taught these young minds that in life they have C = Choices (meaning they can be anything they want, so it was very important to think about what they wanted to become early in life), had to make a plan to A = Achieve those goals, then establish R = Resiliency to bounce back if life challenges caused them to stumble along the way.

Based on the enthusiastic reactions to Dr. Goodson's presentation, it was clear that her passion and caring approach resonated with everyone that heard her speak. These same quality insights are on display throughout *Astronomical Leadership* and will inspire and inform anyone seeking a leadership journey.

LARRY SHAW

Engineer, NASA Johnson Space Center

Houston, TX

Exceptional! *Astronomical Leadership* is not only one of the most inspirational books I have ever read, it is an experience. Dr. Goodson allows you to experience her pain, strength, challenges, passion, growth, and successes to teach and encourage you how to navigate from your current reality to realizing your vision for your life and successively becoming the most amazing you. Her Input, Process, Output program removes any doubt that you can achieve your personal goals, fulfill your mission, and become an effective leader in every domain of your life—work, home, and spiritual. Every word you read, as well as her tools and methods, make sense and are building blocks that lead to a full understanding of the concepts being presented. At the end, you will come to know yourself better, along with identifying your strengths, areas for improvement, passions, distinctiveness, and, ultimately, your future reality.

GWEN ARTIS

Director, International Programs SERVIR

at NASA MSFC/GDR Consulting Group

Huntsville, AL

This is a must-read! Dr. Goodson continues to amaze as she takes her readers on an extraordinary journey through a national disaster, professional challenges, and personal setbacks. Dr. Goodson is a teacher and motivator, and *Astronomical Leadership* will energize and inspire you.

MARVIN CAROLINA JR.
President/CEO, Better Business Bureau
Kansas City, MO

In *Astronomical Leadership*, Dr. Amanda H. Goodson takes you on a journey that exposes you to profound and practical teachings that leads to successful, relevant leadership. Personally, *Astronomical Leadership* has challenged me to maximize my impact as a spiritual leader, father, and husband as she exhorts me to assess the capacity of our ability to create with mind and spirit interacting. Consequently, our thinking can be elevated to the possibilities of that which is greater, to "what no eye has seen, what no ear has heard, and what no human mind has conceived—the things God has prepared for those who love Him." (1 Corinthians 2:9)

APOSTLE WARREN ANDERSON, JR.
Senior Pastor, Living Water Ministries
Tucson, AZ

I believe that each of us have been put on this Earth with God-given assignments. I am absolutely sure that one of Dr. Amanda H. Goodson's assignments was to write this enlightening book, *Astronomical Leadership*. Transitioning from one important phase of my life to another, I found *Astronomical Leadership* a must read. Not wanting to put this book down once I started reading it, Dr. Goodson's storyline of sharing the joys and pains of life and leadership caused me to revisit my past goals and accomplishments, areas where I fell short, and reflect on where I am today while looking forward to the vision and mission of my future. Following Dr.

Goodson's methodology of Input-Process-Output is sure to maximize the potential of any leader seeking to add value to the lives of those in their circle of influence and beyond.

**DR. YVETTE RICE**
President, LLVE, LLC
Decatur, AL

# ASTRONOMICAL LEADERSHIP

## Be amazed at who you are

## Dr. Amanda H. Goodson

*Astronomical Leadership*
by Dr. Amanda H. Goodson
© 2019 by Amanda H. Goodson
All rights reserved.

Edited by Adam Colwell's WriteWorks, LLC: Adam Colwell,
Ginger Colwell, and Dave Ficere
Cover Design by Jaime Anaya
Typesetting by Katherine Lloyd, THE DESK

Published by Adam Colwell's WriteWorks, LLC through Amazon
CreateSpace

Printed in the United States of America

ISBN (Paperback): 978-1-7324474-4-8
ISBN (eBook): 978-1-7324474-5-5

## Dedication
To my family.

To my husband, Lonnie, for his tireless devotion to me, for accepting me for who I am, and for loving me in a way nobody has ever loved me before.

To my son, Jelonni, who also accepts me for who I am, is intrigued by what I say and what I do, and who is seeking his own space to be creative and doing wonderful things across the country. His thoughts are just amazing.

To my mother, Mable, who kept me grounded and also loved me for who I was and brought me to life. To my deceased father, Harold, who inspired me to be an engineer, advance my career, and to think strategically. He made an indelible impression on my heart and mind. In their own ways, my parents made me who I am today.

To my sister, Yolanda, who was there for me as a confidant, a friend, as my lawyer, and as the advisor of my son. I trust her.

# Contents

Input-Process-Output Astronomical Leadership Program
*Transform your thinking, reignite your passion,
and maximize your impact*

# Acknowledgments

When I was younger, Mr. Rodgers was one of my history teachers in high school and never really said much to me or the other students. He just drove us home from school. When I finished eighth place in the math competition, he recognized it. "Wow!" he said. "That was really good." For him to recognize me and be impressed by my achievement was significant. He made me think, *It IS a big deal!*

I also want to acknowledge Wiley Bunn for taking me under his wing at NASA. He sponsored me along the way, enabling me to be successful. It was as though he had my name on his name badge, and when there was opportunity, he offered it to me. He even went back to my high school and researched my background so that he'd know more about me. He threw me in the deep end and watched me swim, then let me know when my strokes needed to be different or better.

Inellia Freeman was in human resources at NASA and helped me smooth out my rough edges. She felt comfortable enough with me, and I trusted her enough, to listen to what she had to say, even with advice on how I should dress and style my hair for success.

Alex Adams was one of my right-hand people at NASA, and I was most grateful for him at space shuttle launches. I could blink or move slightly, and he knew just what I needed or wanted him to do. He took care of everything. Not only did he care about the space program, but he cared about me from a work perspective. Likewise, Regina and Dena, my executive assistants, cared about NASA and me. I am thankful for them.

There are so many others that I could mention from NASA who worked with me on the space shuttle program, and they know who they are. I recognize them for their leadership and support to me to make what we did succeed, as well as for their dedication, their attitude, and their ability to get a shuttle off the ground and get a propulsion system in space to function just like it was supposed to. We had so many flights where their hands touched it, their brain effected it, and their influence helped it. I am grateful for each one of you.

To the people who supported me and put their arms around me in my transition away from NASA to a totally different company and a totally different place in Tucson, thank you so much. Many were very kind to me and to my family, especially Ashley Dickerson, who came with my family from Alabama to help us raise our son into a young man.

All the people at my employer, and people in the community that saw my struggles with the transition, walked alongside me to teach me the do's and don'ts of leadership, management, and mentoring people. They not only held me up, but some locked on with me and we walked together in cadence and rhythm to make things happen. Others allowed me to lift them up and show them a way to be successful.

We can look back and see so many people whose lives were changed tremendously by our partnership, working together, and the influence we had.

Thanks to my current bishop, Bobby R. Best, and Apostle Laura Thompson for their extraordinary leadership and believing in me above and beyond my expectations! I wish to recognize Art Stephenson, who played a pivotal role in my career at NASA. He never changed and helped me to understand the role of a "coach" as a leader. I am thankful for his humility and servant leadership. Dr. Sharese Willis, thank you for giving me the extra push and your help with influencing the "mission" section in this book.

I want to recognize my editor, Adam Colwell, who was instrumental in pulling out of me everything you read in this book. There were some days I didn't really want to talk about it, yet he kept asking the right questions to get me to go deeper in my brain, and deeper in my heart and muscle memory, to create this work. He encouraged me to see that this was going to be useful or helpful to you, the reader, and he stayed steady and true to his craft. He stayed true to honoring me and allowing me to get this out of me in a way that didn't break me, hurt me, or disable me, but propel me.

Finally, what stories I share in this book are related to the best of my memory. The loss of the Space Shuttle Columbia and its crew was very traumatic for me. In writing this book, it pulled things out of my memory I thought I had forgotten because I tried to put out of my mind the pain of the whole ordeal and the transition to Tucson that followed. I thought it would be best to just let it go and start a new chapter in life. Now, I realize that sharing my experiences honestly and vulnerably will not only help future leaders know themselves better, but it will lead them to clean up the frayed ends that were traumatic in their lives—to release them and let them go to make a better life for themselves, for those who follow them, and cause a change in other people's lives.

Let go! Live and love. Be the best person you can be.

Be amazed!

# Note from the Author

The events depicted in this book are related as I remember them. Others may have a different recollection. I did my best not to misrepresent the space program or anyone in any way. I chose, in some cases, not to use individual's full names so as to not put them out front in any way they did not wish.

Chapter 1

# Unlikely Journey

The ring of my phone was jarring as I lay awake in bed. Exhausted and still groggy after too many restless nights, I had decided to sleep in that morning, February 1, 2003. It was a rare respite for someone in my position of leadership.

But what I was about to learn immediately woke me up—and it changed everything.

For me. My team. My country.

"Hello?" I answered.

"Have you been watching TV?" It was my mother, Mable.

"No. Why?"

"I think the shuttle exploded."

Adrenaline surged through my body, my heart drummed in my chest and my stomach sank. "No way. Not on my watch. It couldn't."

Mom's voice was cautious yet gentle. "Please watch, Amanda. I think you'll see." In my shock I didn't respond, unable to even form a word. "It'll be alright, no matter what," she added. "Keep your head up. I know you'll do the right thing."

"Okay, Mom," I said meekly. "I love you."

I ended the call, jumped out of bed, and grabbed the TV remote from the nightstand. Turning on the set, I quickly found CNN Headline News. I stood alone in the room. My husband Lonnie was elsewhere after sneaking out of the bedroom so that I could get some extra rest. My four-year-old boy, Jelonni, was probably playing in his room since it was Saturday morning.

The first thing I saw on TV was a shot from inside mission control at the Johnson Space Center in Houston. I'd been there before, though all my previous official mission control experiences were with launches at Florida's Cape Canaveral. In my role as Director of Safety and Mission Assurance, the first African-American woman to ever hold that position at NASA, I worked out of the Marshall Space Flight Center in Huntsville, Alabama. There my team and I oversaw propulsion systems for the shuttle program with direct responsibility for shuttle launches. We weren't involved with reentry or landings.

The camera was positioned near the back of mission control, and I spied several technicians sitting at their consoles while two others were standing near the front of the room. Looming above all of them was a large wall screen showing lists of data that framed a map of the U.S. with a curving line going across the southern sliver of the nation. That line represented the flight path of STS-107, the Space Shuttle Columbia, as it sped home to land at the Kennedy Space Center in Florida.

Everyone's backs were to the camera, but I didn't need to

see their faces to know that something was wrong. No one was moving. It was as though they were frozen in place, and a sudden coldness stabbed at the core of my being.

Suddenly the television image switched to a dark blue sky punctuated by a glowing light with a vapor trail. It looked like a massive shooting star moving swiftly from the top of the screen to the bottom with a slight right to left angle.

"This video was shot when a loud explosion was heard over Texas," the news anchor reported, her voice professional but noticeably shaky. I stared transfixed as the ball of light suddenly flared before a tinier light broke off to the right of the larger one. Both continued to get smaller in front of the white contrails left in their wake. As the sky lightened to a soft azure, the two dots of light broke up into three. The smallest one disappeared, reappeared, then vanished again. As the larger light divided into even more pieces, I read for the first time the words at the bottom of the screen and tried to process them.

BREAKING NEWS: NASA cannot make contact with Space Shuttle Columbia.

The anchor spoke, "It would appear there's been a catastrophic incident over the skies of Texas. We are seeing huge pieces of metal reentering Earth's atmosphere."

My mind clamored once more.

*No.*

*Not on my watch.*

My phone rang again. I picked it up and answered, instantly recognizing the always serious tone of Alex, my safety and mission assurance integration person.

"Dr. Goodson, have you been watching TV?"

"Yes," I responded. Finding it hard to breathe, I could barely bring myself to ask the obvious. "Is it true?"

"Yes, it's true," he said. "The shuttle has exploded. We need to work the contingency plan. May I have your permission to execute the plan and lock down all of the data?"

I thought of the contingency plan, a big, black, hardbound instruction manual of "What happens if" scenarios. They had already been worked out so that we didn't have to think them through in the heat of an emergency. One of my team's roles was to secure the integrity of the data from any shuttle mission.

I didn't hesitate. "Yes. You have my permission."

Yet even then, after disconnecting the call, I still hoped beyond hope. *There must be a mistake. Maybe it was an airplane. Not the shuttle.* I stood still in front of the TV set, my mind unable to fully wrap my head around what was happening. I was convinced that all the work we had done on the safety of the shuttle and for the souls it carried into space was robust enough. We had learned some harsh lessons from the 1986 Challenger disaster, and while I wasn't in the directorship position back then, I was among those who painstakingly labored to solve the issues that caused that explosion. We had seen so many successful missions since then. In my capacity as director alone, I worked on no less than 35 launches.

Yet even then, after disconnecting the call, I still hoped beyond hope.

But this?

It just couldn't be happening again.

Then my phone rang a third time. It was the integration director for the shuttle program. He told me a meeting was already set at Marshall. I needed to come in right away.

The drive from my home in Decatur to my office at the flight center in Huntsville was about 30 minutes—and it was only then that my disbelief morphed into resignation. I sighed. *My God. This is real.* But I couldn't slide further into dejection. That wasn't an option. Determinedly, I snapped into automatic mode and systematically started compiling who I needed to talk to and what data I needed to gather. I thought through every necessary step to ensure I was going to be ready when I walked into that room to deal with what had just happened. Sentimentality would have to wait.

Still, at a stoplight close to Marshall, I peered up at the sky through my windshield. It was as blue and brilliant as the one over Texas I'd seen earlier on television. The seven-member crew of Columbia, with a mission dedicated to microgravity scientific experiments, was historic as well as heroic. The diversity of the crew was remarkable. There were two women, one of whom was India's first shuttle astronaut; an Israeli Air Force colonel, and son of a Holocaust survivor, who was that nation's first astronaut; and an African-American payload commander.

Columbia's commander was Rick Husband. It wasn't until a couple of weeks later, when I was still just starting to process my sadness and grief, that I recalled the day two years earlier when I first met him over lunch, and the fateful words he shared with me that day.

5

❧

That encounter took place at NASA headquarters in Washington D.C. Safety officers from across the country had gathered there for meetings about new, innovative approaches we were deploying for the safety of the shuttles and their crews. When we broke for lunch, most everyone had gone off in groups, but I was alone and saw Rick Husband also standing apart from the dispersing crowd. I recognized him, of course, but we had never formally met.

I walked over. "Do you want to go to lunch?"

He smiled, an All-American grin if there ever was one, beaming beneath gleaming blue eyes. "Sure," he said. I didn't know if he knew me, but we both were in the same elite NASA family, and that's all that mattered.

We arrived at the little café downstairs where a buffet was being served, found a table, and got our food. I asked about him first, and he told me about the next mission he was preparing for and how excited he was that it was going to be conducting experiments in microgravity. He talked about the payloads that mission was scheduled to carry and laid out his main task as flight commander: to make sure his crew was taken care of while communicating back and forth to Houston, and then relaying anything pertinent to them.

I knew he was the man, the final word when the orbiter was in space. His enthusiasm was evident. Most of all, he talked about his wife, Evelyn, and kids, Matthew and Laura, and how much he dearly loved them.

Then he asked about me. I mentioned that I was married

and had a little boy, and I told him about working on propulsion systems and how, as senior leader for safety and mission assurance, I was one of the people working to get him into space and back safely. More than anything, I wanted him to know how thankful and appreciative I was for what he did as a NASA astronaut—and rest assured knowing his safety, and that of his crew, was my priority.

"The first eight-and-a-half minutes after launch, I got you," I said. It wasn't a cocky statement, but one born from confidence in myself and the ability of my team.

He nodded his head. "Amanda," he said simply, "thank you for doing your best."

Rick Husband was a gentleman and one of the kindest people I ever met. I had no doubt he appreciated and respected me and the duties and difficulties of my position at NASA, and I knew his reply was genuine. But I also sensed that he wanted me to understand that I didn't have control over everything that could happen during the launch or at any other point of a shuttle mission. He, like all the other astronauts I'd been privileged to meet, understood that space exploration was a dangerous business. There was no such thing as a guarantee.

With my pledge, I had put myself and my team on a hook—and it was as if Rick Husband was letting us off it.

Fast forward to January 16, 2003. Just as I had done over the past six years, I arrived at Cape Canaveral as Senior Executive Service (SES) Director to see yet another space shuttle launch, STS-107. I never tired of seeing the violent splendor of takeoff, realizing all the work my team and I had done to prepare for each one.

Launch control at Kennedy Space Center was understandably spacious, a large room with side-by-side station consoles, overseen in front by a massive window with huge louvers. The window was facing toward, but still over three miles away from, launch pad 39A. But it was angled upward so that, from my vantage point, I could not see the pad itself. The architect who built the windows said, "These are the windows through which you see mankind's future," and I couldn't help but feel that spirit every time I peered out of them. There was an elevated floor where senior management personnel were afforded the best view, but the rest of us were positioned below. My team and I were stationed close to the front.

Everyone communicated through headsets, and I had mine on as I sat at my console. On the screens in front of me, I could see both camera images and data readouts, and switch the channels at any time to go from one visual or set of data to another. I looked on as the astronauts—William McCool, Michael Anderson, David Brown, Kalpana Chawla, Laurel Clark, Ilan Ramon, and Rick Husband—suited up and got into the van to ride down the causeway. After arriving, they departed the vehicle and entered the elevator to take them up to enter the shuttle's cockpit. I didn't even think about my past lunch with the mission commander but was focused on the task at hand.

At T minus nine minutes, I heard over the communication system, "Marshall Space Flight Center and Mission Assurance, are you a go for the launch?" That was my cue to ensure that safety was in order and we were ready for blastoff.

"Marshall S-and-M-A is a go!" I announced, as I had many times before. That meant my entire team had given their thumbs up to continuing the launch sequence.

All the other sections of mission control, program managers, and others responsible for the complex space machine known as the space shuttle chimed in, one in another, "We're a go. Go. Go. Go!"

I always loved the sound of those commands.

At just over three minutes before launch, I checked my screen to make sure I saw the shuttle's engines gimbal properly. Gimballing allows the engines to move along with the motion of the orbiter. They were functioning nominally and performing as expected. We waited further, as the excitement built. Moments later, the digital readout on the shuttle clock hit T minus 20 seconds. Everyone quieted in anticipation of the NASA announcer's familiar climactic countdown of the imminent launch.

"We're a go. Go. Go. Go!"
I always loved the sound of those commands.

"Ten. Nine. Eight." All eyes were riveted on the screens in front of them as the tension and anticipation grew.

"Seven. We have a go for main engine start." I saw the red-orange flames jab downward from the orbiter's three engines.

"Three. Two. One. We have booster ignition—and liftoff of Space Shuttle Columbia with a multitude of national and international space research experiments!"

Powered by seven million pounds of thrust, Columbia, attached to a giant external fuel tank and flanked by its solid rocket boosters, shot upward, reaching a speed of more than 17,500 miles per hour. I knew the vehicle and the crew inside were being shaken violently as the rockets consumed an Olympic-sized swimming pool amount of fuel every 30 seconds.

When the vehicle got high enough to see through the window, I gazed up and spied what looked like a little upside-down candlestick, except that the flame wasn't curling upward but plunging downward. Columbia had already rolled so that all of us in the center had a sideways view of the vehicle as it continued its trajectory. Along with several others on the floor, I stood up and craned my neck to watch the shuttle fly higher, and higher still, until it was too small to see. I paid special attention to the plume from the engines. It had a certain color, shape, and consistency that dissipated in a specific way if the propulsion systems were functioning as they should. It looked perfect.

I returned my gaze to the screens in front of me, waiting for the critical point after liftoff called "throttle up." That's when an extra boost of fuel is delivered into the solid rocket boosters, enabling the shuttle to escape Earth's atmosphere at more than ten times the speed of sound. Whenever that command is heard, I can't help but think back to 1986 and what happened to Challenger seconds later.

But I had been on the team that solved that problem. Such an explosion could never, ever happen again. Columbia surged upward and in moments was out of sight and into orbit.

Eight-and-a-half minutes. *We got you!* I thought, and everyone in the center exchanged hugs and high fives.

Before I flew back to Alabama, everyone gathered for the

celebratory post-launch meal of beans and cornbread. It was a time-honored Kennedy Space Center tradition that began after the very first shuttle launch in April 1981, which just happened to be Columbia's first flight. NASA Test Director Chief Norm Carlson started it all with a crock pot of northern beans for his staff. Before long, hundreds of launch team members, managers, and dignitaries were fed from several 18-quart cookers filled with beans. Let me tell you, they were good.

And why not? We were excited and pleased. It had been a textbook launch.

Or so we thought.

The next day, NASA engineers reviewed video footage of the launch and saw something troubling. A two-pound, briefcase-sized piece of insulating foam from the base of the ramp that connected the external fuel tank to the orbiter had broken free 81 seconds after liftoff, striking the leading edge of the shuttle's left wing. For foam debris to break off the tank and hit the shuttle was nothing unusual. It had happened several times on previous missions with little to no significant damage to the thermal tiles that protected the orbiter from the superheated atmospheric gases it was exposed to during reentry. We'd seen this "popcorning" effect on the shuttle's belly and undersides of the wings after previous launches. It looked like chicken pox and created little divots that were repaired after each shuttle's mission was completed.

However, just three months before the launch of Columbia,

a piece of foam had broken loose during launch of the Space Shuttle Atlantis and punched a small hole in one of the booster rockets, inches away from a vital electronics box. An investigation was ordered by NASA because we had never seen a chunk that size and an impact that hard during any previous launch. But the launch of Columbia remained on schedule.

Several days after Columbia was in orbit, I was asked to participate with my team in NASA-wide teleconferences where footage was shown of the foam breaking loose. Opinions were offered, and scenarios were discussed, but in the end, it was deemed that the incident did not pose a "safety of flight" issue.

On the eighth day of the mission, Rick Husband was contacted by mission control in Houston and told about the foam strike but was assured it bore no hazard to the rest of their mission or to reentry. As commander, he then informed the crew and they continued with their duties. A week later, a video taken by crew member Laurel Clark onboard Columbia as the shuttle began reentry showed everyone on board calm, relaxed, and happy to be returning home. There was no evidence of anticipated danger or distress, even as the flashing, hot, orange-yellow gases became visible through the orbiter's portal windows.

"It's really getting fairly bright out there," one crew member commented.

"Yep," came the reply. "Yeah, you definitely don't want to be outside now."

"What, like you did before?" another crew member quipped.

Light laughter followed.

Columbia plowed through the atmosphere at a 40-degree angle, traveling nine times faster than a speeding bullet. The wings heated up to more than 2,500 degrees Fahrenheit, and the only thing keeping the shuttle from burning up in the atmosphere were the thermal tiles that lined its underside and wings. Less than a minute after crossing over the California coast, Houston reported the loss of four temperature sensors on the left wing—the same wing that had been struck by the foam block 16 days earlier. At the same time, observers on the ground saw the first sparks of debris coming off the glowing star streaking across the sky that was the Space Shuttle Columbia.

The orbiter's autopilot fired thrusters to compensate for the disintegrating wing, while videos taken in Nevada, Arizona, and New Mexico all showed more pieces coming off the orbiter. Then Houston reported a loss of tire pressure sensors, and the shuttle performed another roll in response to try to steady the vehicle.

Twenty seconds later, the wing fragmented, sending the orbiter into an uncontrolled spin. Columbia came apart in the air over Texas, just 16 minutes before it was scheduled to land in Florida.

Immediately after the disaster, President George W. Bush activated NASA's Columbia Accident Investigation Board. In the meantime, all of us on the Marshall Space Flight Center Leadership Team used that first meeting the morning of the disaster to walk through what happened with the launch, and examine the mission timeline and what the contingency plan said about our role in the days ahead. I represented the safety and mission assurance perspective and joined other leaders who oversaw the main engines, booster rockets, engineering, shuttle integration, and all other top-level positions at the Marshall center.

It was a day like no other, a real-life drama where I portrayed differing roles. I played the part of the good soldier, overriding all emotion, laser-focused and ready to step in and take care of the tasks at hand. I was the wounded soldier as well, finding private moments to let the sadness come and the tears flow, but always careful to not get down too far. Otherwise, I was going to be useless to the team. Sometimes, I played the frightened little girl, whose only line was to inwardly scream, *Oh my God! What's happening?* Even then, I quickly brought myself back. *You don't have time to wimp out,* I chided myself. *You got to get yourself together, girl.*

That awful day contributed to my later trauma.

My behavior may have been normal, even justified. There was a sense of heightened urgency upon all of us at Marshall and throughout the NASA family. But that awful day contributed to my later trauma. I couldn't let them see me sweat. The problem was, I didn't sweat enough.

When I finally got home that night, I was drained and done. I came in the door and slumped down on the coach. All I could do was sit and stare. When Jelonni came out to see me I put on my brave face, gave him a big hug, and told him everything was okay. That was sufficient for my son, but of course, Lonnie knew me better—and when he saw me, he *knew* better, too. He just let me be, but he also took care of Jelonni and made sure to bring me something to eat, though I don't recall if I even took a bite of whatever it was. I also don't remember how or when I got to bed.

The next day was a Sunday when we'd normally go to church. I was on the ministry team, and Lonnie was an elder at the Macedonia Cumberland Presbyterian Church in America in Decatur. I'd been in church all my life and gave my heart to Jesus at age 12 and had even earned a doctorate in Church Leadership and Administration at United Theological Seminary in 2001. But while I knew much about the Bible and the principles it taught, I had compartmentalized my Christianity. I figured God didn't care much about space shuttles. He was in the church—and so, in general, was the practice of my faith. I experienced it when I was there on Sunday or Wednesday, but otherwise didn't much apply it to anything else. At NASA, there were a few people, other Christians, with whom I talked about God. One of those was Angelia Walker. We often discussed the Lord, messages we heard in church, or something from the Bible. But I don't recall any of us praying for each other, much less the astronauts or the shuttle. The execution of our faith never went too far at work.

That doesn't mean God wasn't working in my life. He was, had been for some time—and would soon direct me on a new path. But right then, the day after the Columbia disaster, I didn't give Him or church the time they deserved. I went in to Marshall early, and we continued our work by looking at all the data beyond the launch sequence itself, placing most of our attention on the external fuel tank. My team and I activated our counterparts in Louisiana where the tank was constructed. We looked at when the hardware was built and where the foam was placed on the tank. We went through every page of every document, looking for any discrepancy or anything that was off. It was all-hands on-deck, including oversight from other governmental agencies to assist us. About two weeks after the disaster I traveled to Louisiana to participate in a meeting with other top NASA leaders conducted by members of the Accident Investigation Board.

After weeks of NASA-directed investigation, our team at Marshall didn't see anything that we had missed. It was a long, iterative process that was laborious and thorough, and I still have copies of the files, notebooks, and photos from all those meetings.

Meanwhile, the Accident Investigation Board continued its work, focusing on recovering debris from the orbiter. Over 20,000 people were sent into a 200-mile long, 10-mile wide swath from Dallas, Texas east into west Louisiana, combing every square foot of land for pieces of the shuttle. Many of those on the team stayed in tents which were set up on the concrete floors of civic centers and other available buildings. In the end, only 40 percent of the vehicle was recovered, but that turned out to be enough. NASA evaluated which pieces were burned, especially those that had a sharp edge from being exposed to extreme temperatures. It became apparent that the left wing (the one hit by the large foam chunk) had sustained the maximum heat damage. The investigation board then decided to conduct a test by assembling parts from other shuttles to construct a life-size model of the wing to test-fire fragments of foam at it.

The gun that was used in the experiment fired a piece the same size as the one that hit the shuttle, simulating the speed and angle they saw on the video footage of the launch. A gaping hole appeared, more than large enough to cause the shuttle wing to disintegrate upon reentry and lead to the destruction of the orbiter and deaths of the crew.

NASA then painstakingly evaluated what could've been done before reentry if they had confirmed a hole was there. Among their ideas were a spacewalk to try to repair the hole or a rescue mission using another shuttle to save the crew while in orbit. When the board finally released the first volume of its findings, it presented what it called a "broken safety culture" within NASA concluding that the agency's Mission Management Team "operated outside the rules even as it held its engineers to a stifling protocol." It was a stinging indictment. When we'd experienced so much success, no one wanted to suggest organizational atrophy. But we had become not necessarily complacent, but comfortable given the criticality of the hardware. The report showed that we didn't have the rigor, that extra edge, to question things more. NASA reorganized and established revised responsibility for safety and quality and brought it back to bear.

The board also charged NASA to come up with a renewed justification for human space flight. In January 2004, President Bush released "The Vision for Space Exploration," mandating retirement of the space shuttle program and replacing it with a new initiative to take humans beyond Earth's orbit to explore the solar system. The first program from this plan, Constellation, was canceled in 2009 due to a lack of government support after the election of President Barack Obama. Today, though, its predecessor, the NASA Space Launch Program, or SLS, lives on through the development of the world's most powerful rocket, created to launch astronauts in the agency's Orion spacecraft on missions to an asteroid and eventually to Mars.

After the Columbia disaster, the next space shuttle flight wasn't until July 2005. The final space shuttle mission took place six years later.

I wasn't there for any of that. Just weeks before the release of the first volume of the Accident Investigation Board's report on August 26, 2003, I had already left NASA, never to return.

But the lessons I learned at NASA were never going to leave me.

Those first few weeks after the Columbia accident were trying to say the least, but all of us were determined to find out what happened and why, to honor Rick Husband and his brave crew. I attended the memorial service on February 4 at the Johnson Space Center in Houston and saw President Bush in person for the first time. He and the First Lady walked right by me on their way to the podium. I was struck by their majestic demeanor, poised and prepared, exactly what you'd want your leaders to portray, as he readied himself to speak. "The final days of their own lives were spent looking down on this Earth," President Bush said of the crew near the close of his remarks.

"And now, on every continent, in every land they could see, the names of these astronauts are known and remembered." It was a poignant, bittersweet day under a sun-splashed sky.

Upon my return, the team at Marshall pulled together and supported one another through the hard work and much sorrow. Especially significant was the presence of my younger sister Yolanda. Loyal, giving, and kind, she had been a constant, faithful presence in my life ever since our childhoods. Slightly over two-and-a-half years my junior, Yolanda was an engineer and a lawyer, and had been at NASA for a decade compared to my 20 years with the agency. She worked at Marshall on propulsion system integration, but in a different department and not on my team or under my leadership. Always even-keeled, she saw everything going on from the perspective of being inside NASA with me. That helped me a lot, even though we only saw each other at work a couple of times a week, usually when we happened to pass one another in the hallways.

It was a poignant, bittersweet day under a sun-splashed sky.

My immediate supervisor, Dave, was deputy director of the Marshall center and managed all of us with precision and compassion. He was a man of faith—and he asked for prayer when he was assigned to go help scour the debris field. I eventually took my turn by assisting the searchers in and around Tyler, Texas. I decided in advance that I didn't want to get out in the rugged, bramble-filled terrain, and that turned out be a wise decision. One of the searchers, a man from the U.S. Forest Service I dubbed "Tiny," showed me the pockmarked blood stains that seeped through his shirtsleeves caused by the two-inch-long sticker briars poking out of the brush and scrub.

In the end, I felt I was going to be of better service by joining others from NASA going out into the community to hand out NASA materials and thank the people of Tyler for their support and concern for our efforts. We took part in a memorial service for the crew with the city's residents and used that opportunity to express our gratitude to all those who had come from across the country to help in the search. I assisted the volunteers when they had questions about any of the shuttle pieces they found. One photo showed me with searchers looking down at a thick, laptop-sized chunk of metal. It still amazes me that no one was injured or killed when the debris hurled down from the sky that fateful morning.

In all, I made three or four trips to Tyler. Each one only fed into my ongoing lament: *Not on my watch.* But the trips also reinforced my belief that NASA was going to find out what caused the accident.

Just before my first trip to Tyler, I remembered the conversation I had with Rick Husband. It was strange. At first, I was thinking about another member of the crew, Michael Anderson, whom I met when we both spoke at a career day for the young ladies attending Spelman College in Atlanta. He was on my mind because I was reflecting on his historical achievement of being one of the few African-American astronauts at NASA. Then, seemingly out of nowhere, my introspection transported me back to the café at NASA Headquarters, and I recalled looking into Commander Husband's blue eyes and hearing him tell me, "Thank you for doing your best," but sensing how he was letting me and my team off the hook.

All at once, all I could think was that I let him down.

Not we. I.

*I let him down.*

From then on, I was heartbroken. I was in shock. I was devastated. I felt like a failure—and that sense of failure consumed my thoughts day and night. Thankfully, I had a protector. Just as he had been that first night after the disaster, Lonnie was strong and vigilant. He intercepted calls to my home from media, friends and family, and others who I hadn't heard from for a long time. Some were caring and thoughtful. A few wondered if I was going to get fired or if I had already lost my job.

It was all so overwhelming. There were days I didn't go anywhere except to and from work. I was quiet and low key, so very different from my usual demeanor. Prior to the Columbia disaster, I brought my "director" persona home with me each day. I was all Type-A, drill sergeant, "you got to get this done," so much so that Lonnie sometimes had to remind me, "I don't work for NASA." Not that he was challenged by any of it. Lonnie was mild-mannered and meek, rarely raised his voice, and was secure in himself and in his manhood. He had been since the day I met him in college. He let me be me—but when I took it too far, he calmly let me know. We understood and respected each other and balanced one another out. We knew our roles and it gave our marriage a firm foundation. Lonnie also saw himself as the priest and fireman of our home. In my hurt and confusion during those trying days, he put out any fires within the family and took care of and nurtured me like I was a little princess.

Mom and Yolanda were there for me, too. They lived together only minutes away from our home and often watched Jelonni at night when Lonnie, who was also an engineer and served as production and operations manager for Daimler-Chrysler, had to work. I either saw Mom or spoke to her on the phone almost every day—and she knew me, too. Aware that I was in a touchy situation, she was careful with what she said or with the questions she asked. Meanwhile, Yolanda remained available to me if I needed her at work or elsewhere.

I appreciated what they were doing for me, and I should've taken advantage of it to allow for an emotional release into the safe haven of their love. But I didn't. I couldn't break down, especially in front of my family. I suppressed it all, and I suffered for it. I ground my teeth so badly while I slept that I woke up each day with a sore jaw. I couldn't sleep for any long periods of time, and I could barely eat.

Most of all, I couldn't figure out what was wrong with Jelonni. He'd watched shuttle launches and landings in the past and even went with me to Florida for a few liftoffs. But now my small, four-year-old son wasn't sleeping either, and anytime I left the room, he cried and clung to me like I was never going to come back. As the TV time and again showed the footage of the shuttle breaking up on reentry, Jelonni looked back and forth—at the set, then at me, then at the TV again, then back at me. It didn't make any sense, but it also didn't get any better, so I eventually took him in to see the doctor.

My son was examined, and then I asked, "So, what's wrong with him?"

The doctor responded, "I don't know. What's happening with you?"

I told him about my position at NASA and the Columbia accident and its aftermath. He shook his head. "He's stressed out," the doctor said. "He's feeling a piece of what you're feeling."

Then I put it together. *My God. Jelonni must think I actually flew in the shuttle. Then, when he watched it crash, he must've thought I was in it, but then he saw me and realized I wasn't, and he couldn't figure it out. He was confused. Scared. So very scared.*

I was, too, but I carried on. Regardless of how I felt, I didn't take a single day off. In my mind, I was going to cope with it all through the work. I never sought counseling for my trauma, received no diagnosis, or took any medication. I didn't even think of those things back then when conditions like Post-Traumatic Stress Disorder were only first being brought into the mainstream.

But I did do something spiritual in relation to what had happened, something I'd never done before or since. For 40 straight days, I decided to get up early, usually around 3:00 a.m., just to spend

I carried on. Regardless of how I felt, I didn't take a single day off.

time reading the Bible and praying until about 6:00 a.m. I may not have thought God had much to do with space shuttles, but I was beginning to consider that He had a lot to do with me.

During that period, He spoke to me. I didn't hear a

booming voice or see some technicolor vision. It was just an unction in my spirit that I knew was Him. He said: "I am going to ask you to do something in 2007 that is going to be the most beautiful thing you could do for me."

I wrote it down and figured it was going to be something big, where I'd be traveling, maybe worldwide. My thoughts were grandiose, but I had no more detail than that.

Meanwhile, in the wake of Columbia, an internal restructuring of the Marshall center was mandated which included my directorship position. Dr. Michael Greenfield, NASA Associate Deputy Administrator, came to Marshall to discuss where else I wanted to go within NASA. He said the organization was looking for the right place to reassign me but didn't want to put me in a role where they felt I wasn't going to be successful. He mentioned several options that he had already dismissed for that reason and said he'd get back to me.

Then, seemingly out of nowhere, I was contacted by an executive search firm hired by an engineering company in Tucson, Arizona. They were looking for someone to help with mission assurance. I took the call and told the person to call me back in a week. I used that time to gather seven referrals for colleagues I thought were ideal for the position. When the firm called back, I declined the offer and gave the person the names of the others. "I need to focus on getting the shuttle back in the air," I said, "so don't call me back. Call them."

The representative of the search firm was astonished. "This has never happened before. We've never had somebody give a job away to someone else. We're going to stay in touch with you. You are very rare and unique."

I hung up and thought nothing more about it. As far as I was concerned, I was staying at NASA. Where else could I go? I was at the highest rung I could get, other than maybe going to NASA headquarters or to Johnson in Houston or Kennedy in Florida. I was in my early forties while my peers were between 55 and 60. I had it good and I was thankful.

Then God did something utterly unexpected. He began to tug on my heart that He wanted me to actually *go* to Tucson. This was unique—the first time He directed me to move from one place to another. But from my study of the Bible years earlier when I got my doctorate, I had discovered that God did talk to people in Scripture and direct them to move, sometimes with no clear reason why. They went along with His leading and great things came to pass.

Still, to have Him lead me to relocate across the country was unusual and uncomfortable, especially considering what had just happened with Columbia. Yet God confirmed His direction and convicted me that I needed to be obedient. I also began to believe that the "most beautiful thing" He wanted me to do was contingent on me being in Tucson. When I told Lonnie about it, he agreed, and we began preparing ourselves.

In May, I contacted the executive search firm that had first called me about the job in Arizona and asked if they still had the mission assurance position available. It had been filled, though not by anyone from my referral list. They did, however, make another position available, and I told them I was interested in being interviewed for it. Shortly thereafter, they arranged for me to go to Tucson. I'd never seen the desert southwest before, and when my plane flew in over the city to land, I looked out the window and thought it was brown, grass-less, dirty, and nothing like what I was used to in Alabama.

When I got to the hotel, God nudged at my heart—again.

"I need you to take another look," he said to my spirit. "I made this place. Nothing about it is ugly."

I walked over and gazed out the window—and I saw beauty emerge right before my eyes: the rolling foothills leading up to the mountains, the green-trunked desert trees, and the tall cactus. Later, when it got dark, I took in a view from those foothills at the glittering city lights. It was as though Tucson was suddenly the most beautiful place I'd ever seen.

I woke up the next day refreshed and went in for the inter-view—which ended up being a series of several interviews with vice presidents and other executives. It took all day, and then I flew back home that evening. As I sat on the plane, I hoped they liked me and had good things to say to each other but, in general, I thought it went well. It appeared to be a lat-eral move, and I was excited to go reinvigorate myself and do great things. I was going to help the world because I was Miss NASA.

I resigned in June and took the month of July off to spend time with mom, who had just undergone knee replacement surgery. I arrived in Tucson the last week of July, and my first day at my new job was Monday, August 4. It had been just over six months since Columbia burned up on reentry.

God set me on my new path. Now I just had to see where it was going to take me.

᪣

Today, that unlikely journey has brought me to a place when I am equipping and training people to become astronomical leaders by helping them transform their thinking, reignite their passion, and maximize their impact through an age-old methodology infused with new life.

It's incredible, really, that I have been given a platform to work with leaders to begin with. After all, my childhood suggested I was going to be anything but a leader when I grew up.

Chapter 2

# Obstacle Course

The common thread woven through the tapestry of my younger years was that I didn't have any confidence. Then again, I suppose I had an obstacle or two to overcome.

I was born in Decatur in November 1961, a time of incredible social upheaval for African-Americans. By then, the U.S. Supreme Court had already ruled against racial segregation in public schools, Rosa Parks had refused to give up her seat on the bus in Montgomery, and Dr. Martin Luther King Jr. and other black pastors and civil rights leaders had coordinated nonviolent protests to oppose racial discrimination. My toddler years saw my state's governor, George Wallace, try to block two African-American students from registering for classes at the University of Alabama, witnessed the March on Washington and Dr. King's "I Have a Dream" speech, and watched the signing of the Civil Rights Act by President Lyndon B. Johnson, preventing employment discrimination. Sadly, it also saw the bombing at the Baptist church in Birmingham, the police attack on marchers crossing the bridge at Selma, and the assassination of Malcolm X.

All were definitively significant events, but I hardly seemed to notice them in the ignorance of early childhood. Born to Mable and Harold Harris, I wasn't aware that my father, who was a Colonel in the United States Army, was able to serve because of President Harry Truman's executive order in 1948 ending discrimination in the Armed Services. I barely remember our brief move to California because of my father's military duties before returning home to Alabama in time to see my baby sister born and for me to start school.

My nickname was Tammy, the name mom originally wanted to give me. But my full name, Amanda Olivia Harris, paid homage to my two grandmothers. I went by Tammy at home and in the neighborhood, but I was Amanda whenever I was at school. To this day, my husband and most of my family call me Tammy.

We didn't have a lot of money and lived in a small, rented house with three very small bedrooms (one of which Yolanda and I shared) and a single bathroom. We often had to stand in line to take our turn using it. We had mice that I often heard scratching about in the walls, especially after knocking on them to get the rodents' attention. There were termites, too, that I sometimes tried to kill by making little holes in the already-thin walls and poking the critters with a knife and fork. Whenever my mom, my sister, and I stayed for a few weeks with my Grandmother Amanda while dad was away on military assignments, I thought it was great, even if I had to sleep on the floor.

Even though it was the norm for us, our church experience was different from most others because my parents attended different congregations. Dad went across town to Kings Memorial United Methodist Church where he was a trustee. Every now and then, for Father's Day or other special dates, we went to his church, but mom, Yolanda, and I always arrived separately from our father. Every time he arrived late, just in time for the benediction, but we knew he was there when we heard his smooth tenor singing. Much later, when dad passed away, mom set his funeral to begin 10 minutes after the hour in honor of his perpetual tardiness to church.

I started first grade when I was five and, at my parent's insistence, attended a newly-integrated school a few miles away from home instead of the still-segregated school just one street over. She felt I was going to have more opportunity at the integrated school, and while there were some other blacks there, it was predominantly white. I was nervous and scared at first because I didn't know what to expect, but I learned to adapt despite my uncertainty. In the African-American community, we spoke using what I called Alabama Ebonics. We cut off certain words and spoke with a distinctive slang. To be understood at school, though, we had to talk like the white kids with their specific southern drawl. I joined up with others from my neighborhood to role play and practice our speech. To fit in at school, we also had to accommodate a plethora of unspoken do's and don'ts that applied only to blacks. That wasn't so much to govern our behavior, but to adjust how we interacted with the white students and teachers. It was challenging to my self-confidence, but that adaptability bred resilience—characteristics, it turned out, that I needed later for similar reasons in college and at NASA, and that have become qualities I now use and teach as a leader.

While I generally behaved myself at school, largely to avoid disappointing my parents, I did tend to talk and giggle too much in the classroom. One day, my teacher put me out in the hall where my cousin, who was a sixth grader, saw me.

"What are you doing out here?" he asked.

"I got in trouble," I replied between sobs.

"It'll be alright," he said. That made me feel better, and from then on, I made sure I didn't do anything to get stuck out in the hall again.

I was kind of unique, a laid-back kid, chunky, and a little weird because I processed things differently than others. I was an analytical thinker who needed everything wrapped up in a nice package. Spontaneity didn't come easily to me. I didn't throw caution to the wind but was calculating in how I took in what was happening around me. I see now that it was a strategy of risk management, another leadership quality I teach today, that manifested itself then in how I related to my schoolmates. I enjoyed being part of the crowd with the other kids, yet I was never really part of the crowd because I was unsure of myself and didn't want to do what they did—even if I did want to hang out with them while they did it.

It was a strategy of risk management, another leadership quality I teach today, that manifested itself then in how I related to my schoolmates.

For example, one of the girls I played with in my neighborhood cussed—a bunch. I thought it was terrible and told her, "Don't do that! If somebody hears you, you'll get in trouble!" Because of what I heard in church, I sometimes threw in, "You'll end up going to H-E-Double Toothpicks." She always responded, "No, I won't. No one can hear me." But her foul mouth didn't keep me from being with her. In later years, I was the lookout scout for couples who wanted to kiss each other. I was with them and made sure they didn't get caught, but I never actually kissed a boy myself because that was wrong. I was often with people who stretched the boundaries, but I mostly stayed within the rules.

Away from school as a little girl, I loved to sing. I was in the Sunbeam Band in our congregation at St. James Cumberland Presbyterian Church. It was a choir with Christian Youth Fellowship that went to other churches or events around town. At home, I sang along to TV show themes and commercial jingles. My favorite show was the Saturday morning cartoon featuring The Jacksons. My mom even took a couple of friends and me to Nashville to see The Jackson Five perform live. Mom stayed with Yolanda up in the seats, but she let me and my friends go down to the floor. We screamed and raised our hands, sang A-B-C 1-2-3, and to this day, I swear Marlon looked right at me. He became my make-believe boyfriend, but my friends preferred that other fella, the little lead singer.

Yolanda and I weren't exactly playmates when we were little. That was partly because of our age difference, but also because she preferred staying in our room with her head stuck in a book, while I was more active. I could be a bit bossy, too, so I think she tended to stay to herself and do different things than I did. That said, we went swimming together at the community pool, and often played games like "Operation" and "Sorry!" though I sometimes quit in the middle of the latter if Yolanda was beating me too badly.

I savored any moments with my father, since he was often gone working on missile systems with the U.S. Army. I remember times outdoors in the driveway helping him fix the car. He changed the oil and other fluids and had me pump the pedal while he bled the brake lines. Dad was the ultimate father. He wanted me to be aware of current events, to read books and the newspaper, and to be an independent thinker. When I did my homework, I often asked him to tell me what something meant. He always told me to go look it up in the dictionary or in our set of Encyclopedia Britannica. He often said "no" to me, too, but that was because he was being protective. It was the way he told me he loved me. I felt a strong sense of direction from him, and we had our moments of tenderness such as when I sometimes rubbed his curly hair for fun, and he always responded, "Tammy, stop acting silly."

Mom worked until dad graduated from college when I was three, and then she stayed at home after that, meaning we saw each other much more than I saw my father. I was just like mom; she'd fuss at me, and I was careful not to fuss right back. I knew it was unwise to talk back to her. Mom was stern. Her parents were stern on her, so she was stern on us. With mom, I knew I had to straighten up and fly right. I thought she was mean, but I know now that mom always had my back. I enjoyed the times she took me to church, and she volunteered with the Sunbeam Band. She got me involved in different things—ballet and tap dance, gymnastics, Girl Scouts—and I had no clue then that she was teaching me to be well-rounded. Serious, calculating, focused, and driven, mom wanted my sister and me to be able to have a different life, to work harder, and to be strong.

Mom didn't let anything or anyone stand in the way of that, either. She routinely showed up at school two or three times a week to make sure I was being treated right, and she was nothing to shake a stick at. Her appearances were famous. Other students would sing-song, "Hey, Amanda. Your mama's baaaack." If someone looked at her and said, "Can I help you, hon?" Mom retorted, "I'm *not* your hon."

As a couple, my parents were quite a pair. I overheard them when they talked about other kids in the neighborhood. They waited until we went to bed and then I heard them chattering in their room like little chipmunks. They even went so far in their conversations to spell words backward, such as "So-and-so was d-a-b" instead of saying "bad," like it was some sort of code I couldn't figure out.

But while their relationship was centered around us, I could tell that they loved each other. They laughed a lot, played card games with one another, and enjoyed hanging out as a couple with their friends. On weekends, dad cooked out on the grill (using his special barbeque sauce everyone raved about) while mom took care of the indoor food preparation. On holidays like Valentine's Day or the Fourth of July, we went on picnics and mom dressed us up in outfits to match the occasion. When dad bought mom assorted candy for Valentine's Day, I took little bites out of the bottoms of the pieces to try to find the ones with caramel and nuts. They knew it was me. Thankfully, I didn't get punished for that, since I did get in trouble for other things like not being in the yard at dark, staying on the phone too long, and—especially—getting bad grades.

In different ways, my parents drove me. Dad wanted me to learn, read, and succeed while mom wanted me to be more disciplined in my thinking. She always told me, "You're going to have to be two times better than everyone else, smarter than everyone else, and do more than everyone else, because they're not going to treat you the same because of how you look." She knew I might be discriminated against and she wanted me to be prepared for it. Because of my parent's determination to push me forward, home was where I felt I had to measure up. That was because my parents wanted me to do better, have better, be better.

Always better.

Mom and dad loved me the best way they knew how, but I didn't always know how to receive it as love. We loved each another and had times of laughter and fun, but I didn't perceive home then as being a "light" place. I often felt weighed down because my priorities were different from those of my parents. Looking back now, I see that my parents were perfect for me. They gave me the opportunity to be adaptive, flexible, and creative in my own way. That pressure was what pushed the diamond forward so that I'm able to navigate life successfully. I could not do that without what they did. They focused on developing my character and competence. They valued most the things I didn't value at that time because I didn't know how important those things were going to be to my future. Back then, my parents did nothing to intentionally feed my lack of confidence. I just wanted to be the good girl, the one who did things right without fail—and I struggled to live up to my own standard of perfection.

This carried over to my studies in school. My teachers did not think I was as intelligent as the other kids, and in my eyes, the color of my skin certainly played into that perception. Even though it was an integrated school, the grading system used was still quite segregated. Students were divided into groups based on academic achievement. Group A was the equivalent of today's accelerated or advanced placement levels. Group B was above average, Group C was average, Group D was below average, and Group F was for those needing special education, crassly dubbed "slow." The problem was the highest any African-American student could achieve was Group C. That was never implicitly stated, of course, but all I knew was that there was not even one black kid in Groups A or B.

I didn't perform well on standardized tests. My mind veered off, and I wondered why so much time had to be spent on them. Still, I made better than average grades in all my courses and felt I qualified for the B group. But if the teachers didn't think I was smart, that was okay with me. That just meant I didn't have to work as hard, though I did do well enough to make sure I met my parents' requirements regarding my grades. I wanted

My self-doubting attitude was that if I flew under the radar, everyone was going to be happy.

to honor what they said about me and expected of me—but I never tried to exceed that. My self-doubting attitude was that if I flew under the radar, everyone was going to be happy.

Throughout school, most of the kids thought they were better than me, so I guess it's no surprise that I got into a lot of fights. They took place away from school, almost like a rite of passage. One time I got into a fight because somebody came up to me and took a bite out of my apple. Sometimes that's all it took. Anything could start a battle. Mom always directed me, "Don't you hit them first. But if they hit you, you better beat their butt!" In my elementary and middle school years, that's exactly what I did. I was bigger than them, and when my temper went off, it was on! I stopped fighting, though, by the time I was 15 because by then the boys were getting bigger than me.

In the end, I just didn't feel like I fit in at school, so I didn't like it much. I felt shunned by the white kids because of my skin color. One time in elementary school, a bunch of white girls surrounded me in the bathroom. "Lift up your shirt," they challenged. "You can't be that color all over! You gotta be white somewhere!" On the other hand, some African-American classmates called me a "cheese eater" because they thought I was better than them when I tried to act and talk like I was a white person. I was also teased because of my weight, and I was tall for my age, too. I often tried to slump down on my desk chair so that I didn't seem so big. I did, however, get a kick out of watching the white kids drink from the water fountain (unlike the grades, it was integrated) after a black person drank from it, but they didn't know it. And I took note of the fact that the water wasn't any different, regardless of who drank it.

As a kid, I had only a few friends. There were Carletta and Margaretta, both of whom went with me to The Jacksons concert. There were also a couple of white girls, twins Charlotte and Sharon. The three of us gravitated to one another because we were overweight and often talked at school, but we didn't do anything together away from there. It just wasn't a good idea.

By the time I hit middle school in the early 1970s, social progress had surely been made, but segregation and racism were still a part of everyday life in Decatur. Being called the N-word out in the community was commonplace, and when mom went to the clothing store, she was sometimes followed around by a white clerk because he thought she was going to steal something. When we eventually moved to a house in a better, all-white neighborhood—the first black family to do so in that area—someone burned something on our front lawn. We didn't know for sure what it was, but it left a big brown spot in the thick green grass.

Mom was a social activist. She took part in protests and marches, something my dad didn't do because he worked for the government. As a teenager, I joined her and loved it. We chanted, "We want our freedom, and we want it now!" and sang about the freedom train moving out. In all, I knew that I was black by the way I was treated. There were certain places I couldn't go and certain neighborhoods that were too dangerous not just for blacks, but for anyone. Overall, I just didn't feel as free as everyone else.

When I started middle school, my parents saw I had an aptitude for math and wanted me to be placed into advanced classes, beginning with algebra. At first, I thought it was funny because "algebra" was the weirdest name for math I ever heard. But because I was black, and perhaps because I was female, the administrators were convinced I was not going to be able to handle it. Mom was clear in her response. "You put her in those classes, and I'll make sure she handles it."

I cried my eyes out when I started the first class, but I did fine. Better than fine. I loved math so much I even played math games by myself.

When I got to Austin High School, I took part in a math competition and won eighth place in the entire school! I was the only girl and African-American in the top ten, and I wasn't even a senior yet. Yet I was shocked when my name was called because I never viewed myself as being smart. Everyone told me I wasn't, and that seeped away my confidence. I never actively sought to be the best I could be. I did try hard in math, though, taking more classes—trigonometry, geometry, calculus—and even joining the math club. I was the only black girl in my math classes.

Outside of math, everything else centered around band. I went to band camp, and my participation excused me from other courses such as physical education—which was fine with me. I played clarinet in the marching band, bass clarinet in the concert band, and piano in the jazz band. Yet even there, my nagging self-doubt surfaced. Whenever the jazz director pointed over to me to do an improvisational solo during a song, I couldn't do it. *You can only play off sheet music,* my mind screamed. *You'll mess it up.* That didn't keep music from fascinating me, though, especially in the way it was composed. When I looked at songs, they had a pattern according to their tempo and beat, and the notes were separated in a certain way. The rhythm might be staccato or allegro, or something more somber. Each sound, each pitch, had an individual purpose. I found music to be just like math in motion, brought to life in the melodies.

I had a couple of boyfriends in high school, but I wasn't that interested in doing everything it took to keep one. I did go out on some dates, but not a lot of them. I wasn't even allowed to date until I was 16. My parents didn't like me dating and I had a ten o'clock curfew, which was different from, well, pretty much the rest of the world! However, I did go to the prom and other dances, and I loved to get out on the floor. Unless I was with a date, mom drove me to the dances, making a point to drop me off as close to the auditorium as possible so people later asked, "Your mom brought you?" It was embarrassing back then but kind of funny now.

As my senior year neared an end, I realized I needed to decide what I was going to be when I grew up—because, incredibly, I was almost there. Yolanda and I used to lay in our beds at night in our room, dreaming about that very thing. I asked, "If you could do anything in life, what would it be?" She said she wanted to travel the world. I then responded, "I want to be on stage." Whether it was as a singer or a musician, I wanted to be a performer—and, more broadly, to be up in front of other people. Later, I came to understand that my desire to speak in front of people, to guide and influence them, was a leadership trait, and it is something I have certainly fulfilled as an adult.

At that time, though, my dream had a decidedly entertainment bent to it. My dad had another view toward my future. "The way you like to live," he told me, "you need to make a lot of money." When he first said it, I wasn't sure what he was talking about. But I did like nice clothes, nice cars, a nice house, and wanted to go do things that were expensive, at least for us. He then added, "You like to live high on the hog." Armed with that perspective, I went to the library to research what professions paid well that might fit with my two interests, math and music. It was clear. Engineers and accountants generally did make money while musicians didn't. So, I thought, *I'll take engineering.* I then made an appointment with a high school counselor.

> That was my first experience with gender bias—and I didn't listen to it.

"Girls are not engineers," I was told, point blank. "Maybe you should go into the military or be a nurse."

That was my first experience with gender bias—and I didn't listen to it. It wasn't that I thought there was anything wrong with being a nurse or in the military. It's just I knew those weren't the path for me. At first, I thought becoming a mechanical engineer was going to be the best option, but then my father offered another nugget of advice. "What about being an electrical engineer?" His suggestion was understandable, considering that was the type of engineer he was.

So that was it. My career choice to become an electrical engineer was official. I was fond of math, and I knew I could make a good living at it.

On graduation night, I didn't sit with the band, but marched in as they played Pomp and Circumstance. I was so excited when it was my turn to get up, get in line, and walk across the stage to get my diploma and have my picture taken. It was a great night, and when I turned that tassel on my hat, I felt important—and knew that since I made it this far, I could be successful at what was coming next. That lack of self-confidence that hounded me back when I started school was now greatly diminished, though I sensed it was still there, lurking in the corner, waiting for an opportunity to rear its ugly head.

I was good enough in band to be offered a small music scholarship to attend the University of Alabama, and I wanted to go there because it was such a big school. My dad, though, was a graduate of Tuskegee University, so that's where my parents encouraged me to go. He loved its smaller size and sense of community and felt I could be successful there. They also knew Tuskegee had a summer pre-engineering program for new high school graduates called Preface. "Try it," they insisted, "and if you don't like it, you don't have to go there."

Two weeks after graduation, I enrolled in Preface. In it, I was tested to determine my aptitude for certain classes—and I placed into the highest of three levels of math courses. When I found out, I said to myself, *Who put me in this class?*

It was the first time—ever—that I truly thought I was smart.

Now I just had to prove it.

Apparently, that wasn't going to be easy.

# Chapter 3

# Confidence Found

On the first day of Preface, I was among about 60 students peppering the seats of the large auditorium in the brick, three-story Tuskegee engineering building. As I scanned everyone, I wondered if I was as wide-eyed as they were as I gaped at my surroundings. *Oh my God,* I thought, *this is it. C-O-L-L-E-G-E! I'm here, with all these smart people, and of my own doing.* Professors and leaders within the engineering school were there to greet us, and at the podium was their head, Dr. Jelani. After a few opening remarks about how Preface was going to work, he got right to the point.

"Look at your neighbor," he said, "to your left and to your right, front and back." All of us looked around, heads swiveling. "Only one out of four of you will graduate. The rest of you will not make it in engineering—so you have to make your decision early if this is what you really want to do. Engineering is not for everybody."

I'm sure he meant the exercise to be a reality check for us, and it was for me. But it didn't scare or dissuade me. It put me on alert. I realized this was serious and was going to be a pivotal turning point in my life. I wanted to make it.

No, I *knew* in my heart that I had to make it.

Self-confidence was blooming within young Amanda Harris.

That summer in Preface was my first excursion into adulthood, and I made some new, cool friends to join me on the journey. There was Gloria from Birmingham, Alabama, gregarious, generous, kind, and loving. She told jokes and took everyone in our group and pulled them in. She was the glue. Complimenting her was Roselyn from outside of Birmingham. She was quieter but still a conspirator with the others on everything we did together. The instigator among us was Felicia from Huntsville. Nobody was a stranger to her, she always giggled, and had the most money in our group, always paying for our food runs to the nearby Chicken Coop restaurant. As wide as she was tall, Felicia was the one who came up with all the great ideas and assigned everyone things to do. She ended up being my roommate for the summer, which made sense since her parents knew my parents and used to hang out together playing card games. I finished off the merry quartet and liked being with the others because they were outgoing and seemed to have a handle on what was happening on campus. Freshmen-to-be, we learned to depend on one another. They were like new family members who refined me a bit while showing me good, clean fun that kept us out of trouble.

We lived on campus in Russell Hall. It was an older building and we laughed that the roaches were so big we could ski on them. Perhaps that was an exaggeration, but it didn't stop us from using boric acid along the floorboards to keep them and the occasional big rat at bay. Pests aside, the rooms were small but comfortable. Felicia and I each had a twin bed, our own closet, and a desk with a bookshelf above it. There was a single window, and the shared shower and bathroom were down the hall. We kept our little refrigerator stocked with sodas, luncheon meat, and cheese, and kept the floor tidy enough to move around without tripping up. I kept my dirty clothes in a big green Army duffle bag and stored anything else in a trunk at the foot of the bed.

As a group, we stayed up late playing cards, talking, and laughing, and often ended up going to sleep in the same room. We were just barely out of high school and in many ways still acted like high school kids, but it was huge for me. I'd never done anything like that before, and it was fun. But that didn't mean I didn't study. With an English course and a pre-engineering drafting class on top of the math courses, I had to. However, the late nights left me tired during the day, and I wasn't used to that. Still, I did well in Preface. I got strong grades, discovered that being proficient in English was important, and that doing math was more fun than I thought. In drafting, I learned to write neatly, use a T-square to make straight lines, and utilize a 3D model to see and draw a building from different angles.

I also became aware of the fact that I couldn't do it all by myself. I had to adapt and get help from the tutors available to us. One of those tutors was named Blessing, and he was one of the smartest guys I ever met. Hailing from Africa, he'd come into our room, dressed in his striped shirt, plaid pants, and stacked platform shoes, snap his fingers, and say with his heavy native accent, "Hellooo—how are you doing?" We'd tell him we needed help. "Yeeees, but eet's a Friday night. You party on a Friday night. Where are you going to partaay?" We'd laugh and then hit the books but loved his flamboyant style.

When Preface ended in August, my grades were strong enough to earn me a full-ride scholarship. It was incredible! All I had to cover were the cost of my books and supplies. During the program, we heard from several speakers whose presentations ignited my interest in the brain and how it worked, particularly in relation to goals. That's when I really started setting them for the first time, and my strategic bent came to the fore. I wrote it all down and mapped it out. I charted how many credit hours I needed to get my degree, what classes I wanted to take each semester and why, how many hours per year that was going to cover, and when I wanted to finish. I took to heart what one of the speakers shared: if you set a goal and have an affirmation of that goal, you have a 97 percent probability of reaching it. That amazed me. *All I have to do is write it down, affirm it by repeating it and believing it, and it'll happen? It's almost too good to be true!* But I adapted to that kind of thinking, it worked—and I'm still doing it today.

When I began at Tuskegee that fall, I was determined to buckle down, starting with an end to the late nights. My scholarship was dependent on me keeping a high grade point average, and I didn't want to lose it. Another motivator was to finish college in four years. In Preface, we were told engineering was a five-year program and that some students stayed in school even longer to get their degrees. I wasn't interested in that. I couldn't imagine staying in college any longer than necessary.

I applied myself—and as I did, I separated myself more from my summertime friends. They laughed at me and bragged about how I was going to be left out when they did this or that, but I was determined. I got myself on a schedule: study until no later than midnight, go to bed, and then get up bright and early, sometimes at 3:00 a.m. if a test demanded it. I didn't pursue Tuskegee's predominantly black band because it played a different type of music, and certainly had different moves when they performed than the mostly white one I had been in at Austin. I did sing in the Tuskegee choir and attended chapel services. But that was it.

I applied myself—and as I did, I separated myself more from my summertime friends.

Perhaps I would've had more fun, and been more relaxed, if I hadn't been so rigid. But I was at Tuskegee for a reason: to become an engineer. I knew it and I pursued it with vigor.

I had two significant people enter my life my freshman year, both of whom affirmed my growing confidence. The first was Janice, my dorm roommate. We shared a room at Olivia Davidson Hall. It was not much different from my summer accommodations with Felicia except that it was further away from the engineering building. The original plan was for Felicia to remain my roommate and we were going to ask Janice if she'd be willing to room with someone else. But after I met Janice, I knew she'd be a perfect fit for me. She came from a nice family in little Jakin, Georgia, was a computer science major, and focused on her schooling. She was a Christian, wasn't a party girl, and had no interest in drugs or drink. Like me, Janice was from a small town and therefore wasn't cityfied and didn't think she was better than everybody else. She was committed to her success and kept her independence, and I found that to be refreshing. Most of all, she was nice, and I could tell that she valued me. We called each other "room," which was fitting since she remained my roommate through our junior years. We talked about our visions for our future, went to the Chicken Coop, Dorothy Hall, and other places together, and enjoyed cooking spaghetti in our room. That first year, Janice became a friend, a confidant, and a trusted partner. I could turn around and close my eyes, and I knew that she had my back.

The second person I met was my first real boyfriend, Craig. We met in one of my engineering classes and I thought he was pleasant on the eye. A black-and-white kind of guy, he was plain, simple, not showy, and wanted the same in a girl. I filled that role for him. The son of an undertaker, he was from Perrine, Florida, a town near Ft. Lauderdale, where his mother was a social worker and his parents were well-to-do. I was attracted to him because of his focus, manners, and gentlemanly demeanor. He was also pursuing a degree in electrical engineering, and we became occasional study partners. We usually did our schoolwork together over in the engineering building because the dorms were too loud and distracting. He walked me back to my dorm, careful to place himself between me and traffic or anything else that could harm me, and sometimes carried my books. Then he left and returned to his dorm in Alphabet City. (We called the boys' dorm Alphabet City because each building was designated by a letter, C, D, and E.) We followed that routine almost every day, and I enjoyed how he made me feel smarter and important. He was a young man of integrity and honor, and I didn't have to worry about him fooling around.

We never really had a formal date before he asked me if I had a boyfriend. When I told him I didn't, he asked if I wanted to be his girlfriend, and I said I did. It was as simple as that. If we did anything outside of studying. It wasn't until later that freshman year that he started to come up to my room to watch TV, and if we were alone we hugged and kissed a bit. I liked that and sensed that he was okay with it, too.

Tuskegee was about three-and-a-half hours away from Decatur, so I was truly away from home, my parents, and Yolanda. At first, I called them about three or four times a week from the lone phone on my dorm floor down the hall. We had to stand in line to use it, then we made a collect call home at a predetermined time, let the phone ring once, hung up, and then waited for the return call so we were not charged for the time. The conversations were light, though I knew if something was wrong I could talk to mom about it. I only spoke to Yolanda if she happened to pick up the phone first. All of them came to Tuskegee on Saturdays in the fall for some of the football games. I enjoyed the games not because I was a fan of the sport but because I loved cheering in the stands and then walking down and around to see all the student groups, the fraternities, and the sororities. It was quite the social event. Afterward, my family and I went out to eat at KFC, which was further away from school than the Chicken

Coop. I appreciated their visits and often missed my family. Sometimes I told dad I needed help with math, and he always came to my rescue. Early on, I went home once a month over the weekend, but after a while that tapered off to every other month. In all, it was an ideal transition from being at home all the time to being on my own.

Interestingly, I decided to run for dorm queen that year. My self-confidence had progressed, and I wanted to try it because it was something I'd never done before. I was still a little chunky and didn't see myself as any kind of beauty queen, but I went for it. Someone told me she were voting for me because she thought I had a lot of nerve running for queen and being overweight. I wasn't sure how to take that, but in the end, I finished second runner-up and got to ride in the back of a flower covered, streamer laden convertible down the main strip of campus for homecoming, all dressed in yellow.

Aside from that, I remained focused on my schoolwork— which was a lot more difficult than I anticipated. I got my first-ever D in calculus, the subject I thought I was most prepared for. In high school, I must've been doing pre-calculus or something similar because the concepts covered in that college calculus class were deeper and more challenging. I was more surprised by and embarrassed about the grade than anything else and thought my parents were going to be upset, but they weren't. They were sure I'd do better the next time around, which was encouraging, even if I grumbled internally about having to retake the class. I also didn't do well in chemistry and decided to drop that class. In my second semester as a freshman, I got a second D in psychology. Dad ribbed me about that. "Don't tell anybody you made a D in psychology," he kidded. "Nobody makes a D in psychology." But I did, and I know why. I didn't do the homework. In fact, psychology was the one and only class I actually skipped, so that I could cook pancakes with my friend Gladys on her electric skillet. I felt so guilty about it afterward. They were the *best* pancakes, though! For all my focus and determination, I still had some disciplines that needed more work, especially regarding certain subjects that didn't engage me. But I also decided that was going to be the last D for me.

Despite a couple of bad grades, I finished my freshman year with high enough marks to maintain my scholarship, and I was pleased with that. It was also time for my first summer break—and another moment that solidified my resolve to succeed, no matter what anyone thought of me.

That summer, I returned home, back to my room that was pretty much the way I left it. I brought along a roommate named Grace whom I met in my math class at Preface. She was different from Gloria, Rosalind, and Felicia in that we were mainly study buddies. We were given so much homework it was impossible to do it alone, so we helped each other with our daily assignments and became good friends. We saw each other every day because we had many classes together and she lived across the hall. From Tuscaloosa, Grace ended up needing a place to stay that summer because she wasn't returning home. We bunked together in my room, and she felt right at home because her mother had been as stern as mine was. I was thrilled mom let her join us, and Grace and I took walks, went to the mall, and rode bicycles together. It was great.

We also went to work at the same summer job. We were hired full-time in the outage division at the nuclear power plant near Athens, Alabama. The jobs came our way purely by accident: the Tennessee Valley Authority sent out letters to selected residents offering full-time positions in Knoxville, and Grace and I should not have received one. When Mom drove us up there for the interview, they apologized but ended up offering us employment closer to home as a reward for our trouble. The drive to Knoxville and back was fun for Grace and me, in that it was the first time either one of us drove a car on the freeway. Mom let us do it and remained patient with me when I kept telling Grace to speed up. She went way below the speed limit, but that was not an issue for me when I had my turn behind the wheel.

It was at the power plant where Grace and I had an unexpected confrontation. It came from a guy named Napoleon. We called him "Nap," and he was a planner in the same division where we worked. He was a good person and, like us, he was African-American, but it turned out that was all we had in common. He wasn't in authority over us, but he felt like he was—a fella looking out for the girls.

"Women are not supposed to be engineers," he told us matter-of-factly during a break. "You won't be successful."

"Women are not supposed to be engineers," he told us matter-of-factly during a break. "You won't be successful, so you should accept that fact and not get your feelings hurt when you aren't successful." Napoleon was as serious and sincere as I've ever seen anybody and truly believed what he told us.

As we drove out of the parking lot that afternoon, Grace was fit to be tied. "Tammy, did you hear what he said? That *won't* happen to me!" It was clear she didn't want to hear it. College was her way up and out.

"I know *that's* right, Grace," I responded.

Right then and there, we vowed we were not going to accept what Napoleon said. Whatever it took for us to be successful, we were going to prove him wrong. Our defiance was going to be his Waterloo!

During the remainder of that all-too-swift summer break, dad helped set me up with my first car. When we arrived at the dealership, I walked right over to a Saab 990. It looked classy, similar to a Mercedes. My father laughed. "You better get on over here to something less expensive, miss high on the hog," and directed me to a brown Datsun 210 sedan. We shared the cost of the vehicle. I paid one-fourth of the $4,000 sticker price. As I drove us home, I knew the Datsun was the right car for me at that moment, and I took good care of it. But I still had in mind the flashier car with bling that someday I'd surely be able to buy.

Upon returning to school to begin my sophomore year, I felt like a light had switched on inside of me, illuminating an important realization: I was a success! Everything my parents had instilled in me was now coming to bear. I settled in with Janice in our new dorm at Russell Hall, found out where all my classes were held, got my books and supplies, and went to it. Nothing was going to hold me back from being an electrical engineer—and on my timeline!

During my second year at Tuskegee, I got more involved in singing. I was in two choirs, both as a second soprano. The college choir performed every Sunday morning in chapel with a mix of hymns, an occasional gospel song, and traditional Negro spirituals. I also sang in a gospel choir not connected to the college that traveled around to local churches and performed contemporary gospel music. This first tangible expression of what I heard and learned in church during my childhood also birthed within me a desire to read the Bible. I even began attending Bible studies in the campus chapel, learning about how Jesus is the Son of God and that those who believe in Him will be saved. One of the things I discovered in my reading and study was that my mindset was not focused on my relationship with God as much as I felt it needed to be, in part because I was putting more attention on my relationship with my boyfriend. Because of that, I decided to break up with Craig. I was convicted that we were doing something wrong because we were spending so much time together. It was hard because I really liked Craig and desired a long-term relation-ship, but there was something deep inside me that wanted to be righteous before God and not offend Him. In the midst of that decision and my early spiritual awakening, my classes were still plugging along nicely. I enjoyed my studies and got great grades—even when I sometimes slept in and missed a morning class because I'd been up late studying the Bible and worshipping. God's grace was always upon me.

That summer when I returned home, Grace came to stay with me again and resumed her employment at the power plant, but I got a different job. It was at the Champion Paper plant in

Courtland, Alabama, about 20 miles away from Decatur. My main role was to update and fold electrical drawings. They were stored in a repository and had to be kept nice and neat. I made sure the lines were straight, the edges were sharp, and the creases were smoothed out. While there was no one there to stink up the work culture, the place did smell bad. Think of rotten cabbage, and then imagine me getting a whiff of that as I got closer to the plant and carrying that stench home with me on my clothes and in my hair. I had to shower and change the moment I got home each day. But it paid double what I made at the nuclear power plant, and I ended up returning to that aromatic job between my junior and senior years.

By the start of my junior year, I began being rewarded more for my good grades. I was inducted into Eta Kappa Nu, the honor society for the Institute of Electrical and Electronics Engineers (IEEE), an association dedicated to advancing innovation and technological excellence that today remains the world's largest technical professional society. IEEE allowed me to have more interaction with faculty and get invited to key in-house engineering activities. I was a champion and ambassador for the Tuskegee engineering department, so that when companies like Proctor and Gamble, Lockheed, or Hughes came to the college, I greeted the visiting executives and prepared them for their presentation or event. We went on different outings to represent the school for lecture series, met to discuss initiatives to help our fellow engineering students, and provided mentoring for them. As a senior, I became the honor society's vice president and was also involved with the National Society of Black Engineers. That enabled me to be involved in events such as science fairs and to visit schools to talk to high school students about math and engineering.

Being in these organizations was my social outlet, and I helped lead other students by bridging the gap between them and the obstacles they faced. Working together, we came up with creative, strategic solutions to their challenges. All this fed and nurtured my leadership expertise and capabilities.

Because of all this activity, I essentially had no social life outside of school—except for starting to date Craig again. During my continued Bible reading, I came to the realization that I could not be sin free. That allowed me to make room for the time I spent with Craig and the way that he made me feel liked and needed. I concluded that our relationship did not undermine my relationship with God. I also continued with the Tuskegee choir and kept reading my Bible. I wanted to know more about God while also understanding that I didn't need to be perfect but could be human and still accepted by Him.

Between my junior and senior years, I worked at the paper plant, hung out with Grace who stayed with us for a third consecutive summer, and kept in touch with Craig by phone or letter while he was back home in Florida. As we communicated, we decided we wanted to get engaged. He was working for a roofing company and said he had saved some money for a ring. I went over to Mitchell's, a wholesale and resale jewelry store. I found a lovely band, custom made by the jeweler, with a one-fifth carat flat stone that looked bigger than it really was. I sent him a picture of it, and he told me to buy it. It cost $170. There was no formal proposal, nothing romantic. Craig and I weren't like that. But my family was happy because they liked him. We were in no rush to set a date, though. He was one year behind me in school, and we agreed we weren't going to get married until after he finished college.

While that was happening, I wanted to work ahead academically and took a history class at nearby Calhoun Junior College. I realized during that class that if I had done the same thing my previous summers, I could've graduated early. Even more driven to finish, I couldn't wait to get back to Tuskegee for my final year and to be a senior. That was also the year Yolanda joined me at college for her freshman year. I checked in on her every now and then to make sure she was getting along okay. But I was busy, especially when I started going out for as many job interviews as I could get, so we didn't see each other often.

My senior year flew by and before I knew it, it was over. My four years at Tuskegee reframed who I was by teaching me how to lead, influence others, and like myself more. It also allowed me to develop a wider view of the world by seeing that people offer value in different ways. It taught me both interdependence, by discovering I could work hard with and depend on others, and independence by realizing I could be on my own and be okay.

My four years at Tuskegee reframed who I was by teaching me how to lead, influence others, and like myself more.

I left school with a bachelor's degree in electrical engineering. More than that, I left Tuskegee with confidence.

Amanda Harris was all grown up and ready to make an impact—and I already knew where I was going to start!

# Chapter 4

# Bold Proclamation

Through Tuskegee's job placement assistance, I had no less than four employment offers waiting for me upon graduation. Two were with Hughes and with the U.S. Air Force, both in Los Angeles. The third was with the U.S. Army in Huntsville.

The one I chose, though, was NASA. Not only was it also close to home in Huntsville at the Marshall Space Flight Center—but it was *NASA!* I'd always thought of our nation's space program as this amazing place filled with smart, cool people. I studied up a bit about space shuttles, was fascinated by them, and was excited about being part of a culture of innovation that helped us get into space and kept us there. NASA also gave me the opportunity to have a career distinct from my father's. I wanted to be difficult.

My interview for the NASA opportunity was via two phone interviews. The first, with the test and evaluation branch chief, covered the usual questions about my education and my perceived strengths and weaknesses. I was also asked about how

I'd feel working in the test and evaluation branch. I was told I was going to work on shuttle payloads, fabrication of test equipment and the quality assessment of that equipment, along with x-ray and ultrasound testing of various aspects of the shuttles. I thought it all sounded exciting! The second interview, with the test and evaluation division chief, gave me an opportunity to ask more questions about what I was going to be doing and learn about where I was going to work at the Marshall Space Flight Center.

Not long afterward I was called and given an offer. I accepted it without hesitation.

I was hired on June 6, 1983 as a professional engineering intern in the test and evaluation branch. It paid an annual salary of $21,500, which was cool, even though I knew friends from college who were making more with other non-government employers. Nevertheless, I was an engineer, and that was all that mattered. Some chose engineering to be able to design things, but I was an engineer so that I could lead and make a difference.

Craig was happy for me and we saw each other a couple times a month on weekends as he started his senior year at Tuskegee. In the meantime, I moved back in with my parents until I could get an apartment, and mom helped me buy the clothes needed for my position. I already had some nice business suits purchased for my job interviews, but for NASA I needed more high-quality outfits that were made to last a long time. We bought suits that were blue, black, and charcoal grey with white, pale pink, and pale blue blouses, all conservative yet sharp. We added comfortable dress shoes and a string of pearls to show elegant femininity.

On my first day at Marshall, I went to the test evaluation branch group to fill out mounds of paperwork, then went to the high bay area where I was given a tour with different people showing me the various departments where I was going to work. I was the first African American *and* first woman engineer in that group, so I got some funny looks, but most everyone was polite and professional. It helped that there was already a black female secretary there named Nancy who was feisty and well respected.

The fact that I was the first engineer there of my race and gender was significant to me, and it created an inner tension that brought back mom's words from my youth: "You're going to have to be two times better than everyone else, smarter than everyone else, and do more than everyone else … they're not going to treat you the same because of how you look."

The fact that I was the first engineer there of my race and gender was significant to me.

I was grateful to be at NASA, but I was also a bit nervous. *These people are smart*, I mused. *But I must've been smart enough to be hired.* My self-confidence was intact because of what I had achieved in college, but I also had no idea how far I could really go at a place like NASA. More than anything, I wanted to add value to what was happening at the space agency—and do it right away.

As I took my place each day at my desk in the bullpen, an open area with cubicles separated by light brown, burlap-like partition walls, my new coworkers started peeking over and around the barriers and saying hello. Among those I met those first few weeks was Jim. Hired to the same engineering intern position but not sharing the same roles, he had a leg up on me because he had done some summer work at NASA earlier. I quickly identified him as someone I needed to know because I figured he knew more about what was going on there than I did, and I wanted to learn from him. As we got to know one another and discuss our goals and what our futures may hold, he became a friend. Jim was also direct and truthful to a fault, which is why I shouldn't have been surprised by what he said one afternoon as we visited in the hallway near the bullpen.

"The only reason you're here is because you're black. You know that, don't you? It's part of affirmative action."

"That's not true," I countered.

"Yes, it is. Go ask somebody. They'll tell you."

I knew he wasn't being mean, and certainly not racist. He was just telling it like it was, at least from his standpoint. But for me, it was the same thing all over again. The teachers back in elementary school. The administrators in middle school. The counselor at the high school. Napoleon at the nuclear power plant. Another voice suggesting that my race or gender, not my qualifications, was what got me this far. Was what defined me. And I was getting tired of it.

I rolled my eyes and sighed. "Well, we'll just see about that, Jim," I said. We parted, and I considered going to my boss at that time to see if the whole affirmative action thing was true. But I never did. It didn't really matter. I was there—and Jim's words simply gave me renewed motivation. *You don't have me. You don't control me. I'm a black girl from Decatur. I'm used to people talking smack about me.*

I wasn't going to let Jim, anyone, or anything define or deform me.

I worked hard through my first year, seeing NASA as my proving ground and embracing my work with gusto. When Craig graduated from Tuskegee, he found an engineering job in Huntsville. Later that summer, July 1984, we followed our plan, got married, and moved into my apartment. Our time as husband and wife instantly mirrored what our relationship had always been—we focused on our jobs and saw each other only in passing. We were far from blushing newlyweds. We were two engineers, we thought like two engineers, we acted like two engineers, and our marriage reflected that (no offense intended to engineers). We were a functional couple that acted functionally toward one another, but we never progressed beyond that. We enjoyed each other's company, but we were naïve. We really didn't know how to have a real relationship. There was little spontaneity, little playfulness, and little spark. It just wasn't in us because it never had been.

NASA, though, was far more engaging. I took part in one interesting project after another. Among them was an isoelectric focusing experiment to be used on the space shuttle. It was designed to take all the constituents of human blood, separate the white and red blood cells, freeze them in a vacuum, and then return them to Earth so doctors could use them for research. I was chosen to represent quality and mission assurance on the project and report back to its director, Wiley, as the project progressed. Wiley was a slightly balding fellow who always smoked a pipe, usually protruding out of the side of his mouth. Sometimes brash in his tone, he was smart, and unlike most other high-ranking supervisors I met, was genuinely concerned about learning more about his employees other than just their immediate job duties. He often pressed us about our goals and ambitions, and while his brusqueness offended some, it didn't bother me at all. In fact, I rather liked him.

He called me in one afternoon to give him the latest update on the experiment. It wasn't the first time I'd been in his office, but I was still taken aback by the sheer size of it. I could do several cartwheels and backflips and not even come close to hitting a wall or ceiling. I guess the space was fitting for one holding his position: Director of Quality Assurance, to be expanded later to Safety and Mission Assurance.

I sat down across from him at the massive conference table. He took a puff from his pipe.

"What do you want to do?" he asked.

"What do you mean?"

"I mean, what do you really want—here at NASA?"

I thought about it and heard a voice within exhort me. *Be bold.*

I leaned forward in my chair. "I want your job."

He blew out a billow of smoke and laughed as if he were thinking I had no idea what I was asking.

"You want my job?"

"Yes, sir!"

He swiveled in his chair and looked straight ahead, as though assessing me as much as his response. His gaze wasn't skeptical, though. It was credulous. Respectful.

"I want to take you seriously," he said. "As a kid, I was taught to throw rocks at black people. I knew that wasn't right." Another puff on the pipe. "I've been looking for someone to help, to create a legacy." He paused. "Okay. If you want my job, you're gonna have to work hard, do the jobs you never want to do, and do the jobs others are not willing to do."

Suddenly, I was the one challenged to take him seriously. Was he really going to give me the chance to go after his position? "I can do all those things."

He got up from his chair, and I rose from mine. "All right, then. I've got some work to do to make this happen. And no complaining from you, okay?"

"Yes, sir."

As I left Wiley's office, my mind was buzzing. *I need to do what others can't. Do what others won't. Find a space where nobody is and cannot touch where I am.*

As I headed back toward my cubicle, though, I also thought, *Girl, what did you just say?* I took a quick detour and found Inellia. She worked in human resources and had set herself apart as someone I could go to for advice, much like a personal coach who gradually had become my NASA mother. A fair-skinned black woman, Inellia had a ready smile, was quiet and meek, and possessed a humble boldness. She looked out for me and always had a word on how I could do something differently or better. Really, she helped me to write the rulebook for myself, to shape and reshape my thinking.

I told her everything that had just happened with Wiley, including my bold declaration to take his job someday.

"If you're gonna do that, you really need to listen to what

he says." Then she grinned. She didn't explicitly state it, but because of her position in human resources she surely knew I'd be the first black woman to ever hold that directorship position. "The impossible might be possible."

She gave me a few more words of advice that let me know what I had to do. I left her office thinking, *I need to look the part, dress the part, and think the part. When opportunity meets a prepared person, there's no stopping them.*

I returned to my cubicle, sat down at my desk, and pulled out my engineering notebook. I then wrote down some goals related to what could happen if I had Wiley's job. *I got into engineering to lead, to influence people,* I reminded myself. *This will let me do exactly that!* The pen just flew across the page, I was so enthused. Then I sat back and took in my small desk and the partitions boxing it in, then gazed up the beige wall to the harsh fluorescent lights in the ceiling—and knew this wasn't going to be my place forever.

I began to dream about what could be.

True to his word, Wiley started giving me projects. Some of them I didn't like and indeed probably wouldn't have chosen to do. He sent me into meetings where I had no idea what to say or do other than take notes on anything pertaining to quality and mission assurance and bring them back to him for review. In these meetings, I felt like a non-swimmer being thrown into the deep end of the pool with nothing more than little floaties around my arms. Other tasks were those I was certain no one else would've wanted, like when he sent me into test areas to help assess how hardware and equipment scheduled to fly in the shuttle's cargo bay reacted to vacuum or weightlessness. I often had to wear special equipment similar to what I often wore at my previous job at the nuclear power plant. That wasn't a problem for me, but I knew others who didn't want the bother or the risk of going into the sometimes potentially hazardous testing areas.

I also continued participating in experiments on behalf of the shuttle. Basically, whatever Wiley told me to do, I did it without question. With each assignment, he wanted me to show him my findings and share my perspectives. He always asked, "Why did you do it that way?" or "How could you have done that better?" I often did mathematical assessments by hand for him and he challenged my assumptions. He questioned the processes I chose and the tools I used. Anywhere he found a hole, he exposed it and pushed me to close it.

Push, push, push.

Because of the commitment I made to him, Wiley never held back. I wanted his job? He was doing everything he could to prepare and position me to have it. With every critique, he expressed how he was pleased or impressed with my efforts. He also gave me life lessons that related to my professionalism or to leadership, such as to never bring a problem forward without already having thought through a potential solution for it. Piece by piece, Wiley fed me the sustenance I needed, salting and peppering me, seasoning my expertise and flavoring my growing leadership skills. After leaving his office each time, I went to my desk and made copious notes, capturing every morsel of wisdom. Rather than have him question my numbers or processes, I wanted to anticipate his queries even before he asked them and have ready responses. I wanted to *think* like him.

Both Wiley and Inellia saw hunger, integrity, and even an innocence within me, qualities that, combined with my developing skill set, identified me as a leader. They worked to marry potential with opportunity to create purpose. Wiley especially appreciated that when he gave me corrections, I made the changes without complaint and without ever saying that what he was asking was too much for me. It wasn't. I was determined to do whatever it took to succeed. I was young, and I didn't have all the answers, but I gradually started to reason like him. I began thinking like a senior leader—surmising and even anticipating his approaches to solve problems. As I did, the dream grew, and I gained clarity.

I also added action to those dreams. As I interacted with Wiley and others in authority, I realized I had to change the way I spoke. Just as I had done back in school by learning to talk like the white kids, I began to augment my speech. *It's not enough to think like a leader*, I told myself. *You have to talk like one, too.* I recorded myself on cassette and listened in the car driving back and forth to work. I spotted weaknesses and practiced my enunciation. For example, instead of properly saying the word "fiscal," I always said "physical." So, I repeated it and other words like it until I got them right. I worked to improve my communication in other ways, too. In one meeting, I noticed Bob, a German chief engineer who designed rocket engines, reading from three-by-five index cards he carried with him in his shirt pocket whenever there was a lull in the meeting.

"What do you have on those cards?" I asked.

He held a few of them out to me. I saw the small but legible handwriting in ink. "These are formulas for the engines," he said with his decidedly staccato accent. "Designs like this used to be drawn up on napkins or with paper and pencil. I read these again and again so that I know them."

I was learning to take someone else's best practice and transform it to make it work for me. I got a package of cards and started carrying them with me. Whenever I heard a leader say something influential or use a power word or phrase, I immediately wrote it down. Later, I played games with myself using the cards, putting tick marks on each one every time I used what was written on it, or using them like flash cards to retain and memorize a term like "off nominal condition." I created ways to make that content my own, transpose it to increase my knowledge, and improve how I presented myself to others.

In addition, I wanted to remove every hint of doubt, every element of conjecture or perception—not from my thinking, but from the minds of those around me. To have a seat at the table, I felt like I had to prove myself. I also had to overcome the impression from others that I was not qualified to be doing what I was on behalf of Wiley.

To have a seat at the table, I felt like I had to prove myself.

This led to some unexpected pushback from my colleagues. We'd discuss a certain project and I'd offer my perspectives, insisting that we should do something differently or consider another methodology. Then I'd learn they were getting mad at me and talking behind my back, saying, "Who is *she* to come tell us what to do." I wasn't trying to dictate or offend. I simply wanted to help, add to the process, and improve it. But I wasn't received that way. Whether it was because of my youth, inexperience, gender, race, or a combination of all of them, I was being shrugged off, even disregarded.

I finally took the matter to Inellia and her counsel surprised me.

"If you tell them one more thing, I'll stop talking to you."

She explained that they weren't appreciating, much less receiving, the value I was bringing to them and that I didn't need the frustration if they were going to dismiss me. So, just as I had done in college, I began to separate myself from the others. I understood that if I rode their wave, it wasn't going to take me out as far as I needed to go. I had to stick my neck out to beat them by a nose in everything I did. This included making sure I was being noticed without making my efforts obvious. Depending on the situation or meeting, I wore a slightly different colored blouse or an extra string of pearls. If I wanted to communicate experience, I wore my hair in a bun. If it was creativity I felt they needed to see, I kept my hair down over my shoulders. At Wiley's insistence, and with the added exhortation from my father, I also began working on my master's degree. It all started to open up the aperture for me to see what was placed in me that was not placed in others.

When Wiley was away from his office, I even started going in there, alone, imagining myself in his job, creating a future in my mind. Calling those things that be not as though they were.

I was not going to let this door shut. I was not going to let this opportunity pass me by.

I was being set apart.

Prepared for something bigger.

I just could never have predicted what was going to be the catalyst for that something.

As 1985 came to a close, so did my brief marriage to Craig. Our regimented relationship ground to a halt, and as it did, we separated, and I went back to my parent's house. Once there, I moved into the same bedroom I had when I left for Tuskegee over six years earlier. I brought a few basic belongings and sought to displace my guilt over the failure of my marriage with an even greater focus on my career. I dove in deeper than ever and served on a variety of assessment, inspection, and auditing teams, all under Wiley's watchful eye and Inellia's dutiful support. I was tasked to identify problems and then creatively strategize solutions in an organized but creative fashion, so others could see what I was communicating in a way they never had before. That was my distinctive.

The last week of January, I was away from my office at NASA and in a hotel in Huntsville for a set of training classes. Such off-site training was not unusual, and even though that Tuesday morning was the next shuttle launch, I wasn't really thinking about it. Oddly enough, even though much of the work I did those first two-and-a-half years at the Marshall Space Flight Center served the shuttle program, I had watched only a few launches. Even though this launch had garnered more national attention because it was going to be the first one to take a civilian into space, I couldn't see it anyway. I was in the training class along with nearly 200 other workers from throughout the Huntsville business community, and away from the televisions in the lobby.

Then a woman burst into the conference room. It was almost a quarter to noon.

"Breaking news!" she shouted. "The shuttle blew up!"

*What?* My mind struggled to comprehend the possibility of such a disaster, much less accept its reality. *You've got to be kidding me?*

The instructor put the class on hold, so we could head to the lobby to watch the news coverage. Most everyone was silent as the replay of the launch began on CNN, so much so that we could hear the audio. I started making out the commentary shortly after the shuttle had cleared the tower.

"Breaking news!" she shouted. "The shuttle blew up!"

*"Good roll program confirmed. Challenger now heading downrange ... Engines beginning throttling down now, at 94 percent. Normal throttle's, uh, for most of the flight is 104 percent ... We'll throttle down to 65 percent shortly...*

My heart was pounding. In my limited knowledge of launches, everything looked and sounded normal.

*Engines at 65 percent, three engines, uh, running normally, three good fuel cells. Three good APUs ... Velocity 22 hundred 57 feet per second, altitude 4.3 nautical miles, down range distance three nautical miles ...*

I kept watching—waiting.

*Challenger, go at throttle up..."*
*"Roger, go at throttle up..."*

At that moment, there was a fireball, followed by gasps and cries of "Oh my God!" or "Oh no!" from those with me in the lobby that drowned out the audio. But I didn't say anything. I just stared at the contrails of what I knew had to be the shuttle itself raining downward toward the ocean. Those held my attention more than the zig-zagging booster rockets flying askew and away.

Rockets that were no longer flanking the fuel tank. No longer propelling the shuttle toward orbit.

After several seconds, the audio returned.

*Flight controllers here looking very carefully at the situation...Obviously a major malfunction...We have no downlink.*

Then, after another long pause as debris plummeted down from the sky.

*We have a report from the flight dynamics officer that the vehicle has exploded. The flight director confirms that. We are, uh, looking at, uh, checking with the recovery forces to see, uh, what can be done at this point.*

As the coverage returned to the news anchors, I tried to keep watching, but couldn't. Everyone started talking, and some, who knew I was there from NASA, began asking me all kinds of questions. I had no responses because I didn't have the background or expertise to provide the answers. I had been in some pre-flight or post-flight meetings at Marshall regarding shuttle missions, but only as a spectator, not as an active participant. I'd never worked a launch and didn't know detail about launches. Therefore, I couldn't accurately speculate, much less know, what went wrong with Challenger.

All I knew was that it was gone. The shuttle—and its crew. Gone.

The class reconvened, and it provided a welcome distraction from the disaster. It went on as scheduled until 5:00 p.m., after which we all headed home for the day. I hadn't called anyone at Marshall, hadn't contacted anyone in my family, and no one had called me. But as I drove home, I couldn't help but wonder, *What does this mean for NASA? For our jobs? My goals?*

*What happens next?*

I had no idea.

When I arrived at mom's, it was obvious everyone there knew what had happened. They asked if I was okay and wanted to know what I knew, though they understood I likely didn't know much. We watched the continuing news coverage, viewed the disaster once more, and conversed about it—but there were no hugs, no kisses, no tears. I didn't even hear from Craig until later that week when he called, curious about my well-being.

When I went to bed, I thought about what I was going to face the next day. Was there going to be heightened security? Do I go to my same building like always? I knew there were contingency plans for such an event and assumed it wasn't going to be business as usual. But I did get to sleep quickly and rested fitfully.

That was good—because nothing was ever going to be the same again.

# Chapter 5

# Declaration Realized

The next morning, I went back to Marshall and got to where I needed to go without any problem. If there was added security, I couldn't tell. What was obvious, though, was that there were a lot of sad and hurt people. Others were angry, sullen, quiet, or reflective. We came together that day expressing sorrow and empathy for one another. I went to Inellia, and after confirming I was okay, she gave me her usual encouraging wisdom.

"Keep your head," she said. "There may be some opportunities for you out of this. Be ready."

I couldn't imagine at that moment what those opportunities could be since we were on stand down, meaning no new work having to do with the space shuttle program was going to be done that day, or likely for a long time to come. But speculation was already circulating, particularly from those who did work on launches, about what happened. The talk focused on two things.

Was it too cold to launch?

Did the O-rings fail?

It wasn't the first time I'd heard about O-rings, the circular gaskets that kept gasses from escaping from the solid rocket boosters. But I knew nothing more about them than that. They'd never come up in any of my previous work on shuttle payloads and experiments.

The next few days at Marshall were much like the first after the disaster. I never saw Wiley during that time because he was already well involved in the primary investigation of the accident. Before long, though, we were put to work helping with data capture and getting plans and documents on anything and everything ready, just in case Wiley was going to need them. My area was well removed from anything having to do with the solid rocket boosters, but I still joined my colleagues in combing through flight data from the Challenger payload and other electronic information, looking for that needle in the haystack that could've contributed in any way to the disaster.

I occasionally interacted with Wiley, but it was all-hands-on-deck and stayed that way for nearly two years. We examined. We analyzed. We assessed. We worked—hard. After a while, we started projects on shuttle bay items for the next flight, whenever that was going to be. My job was all-consuming, and I thrived. I worked on my master's program and began taking additional classes on leadership while continuing to set myself apart from my colleagues. I was motivated by standards, goals, strategies, and tactical execution at a greater level than those around me. For many, their jobs were a means to an end to simply be involved in the space program, earn income, and accumulate vacation time. For me, my job was everything; it *was* me. Therefore, little of significance happened in my personal life during that time. I once again moved out of my parent's home into an apartment, and I settled into a routine of hanging out with friends, mostly from work, on Friday night, playing games or watching movies at their houses. Saturday was for sleeping in and running errands while Sunday was for going to church. I had a work life, a friend life, and a church life, and I compartmentalized one from the other. Spiritually, I was still applying biblical principles to my life but wasn't pursuing anything deeper. Since Craig, there had been no man in my life, and I didn't date much. I wasn't interested in a relationship and certainly didn't have the time for one.

From February 1986 through late 1987, return to flight was the all-encompassing focus for NASA. President Ronald Reagan announced the Rogers Commission that began reviewing the circumstances surrounding the Challenger accident in order to recommend corrective action and report back to the White House. Within days of the disaster, NASA investigators pinpointed a rupture in a field joint of the shuttle's right solid rocket motor as the likely cause of the accident. Commission members, though, were more disturbed to discover that engineers from Morton Thiokol, the firm that manufactured the solid rocket motors, recommended against the launch of Challenger the night before the disaster because of the cold temperatures at Florida's Kennedy Space Center. However, those engineers' managers—apparently pressured by top NASA officials at Marshall—overruled their concerns. It was also revealed that more senior NASA officials had no knowledge of this.

The Commission then ruled that the NASA team working with them could not include anyone involved in the decision to launch. Even more, the Commission escalated its investigation to scrutinize NASA management practices and chain of command protocols. By the time the Commission submitted its report to the president on June 6, leadership changes had occurred at the top levels of NASA, including at Marshall, but I wasn't impacted by any of those alterations. My work continued at a steady pace as we worked on several of the thousands of items NASA identified as being critical to return to launch.

The first of the eight recommendations from the Commission called for the faulty solid rocket motor joint and seal to be changed through a new design eliminating the joint or a redesign of the existing joint and seal. Some of that work was going to be done by a team based at Marshall in cooperation with a group of engineers from Morton Thiokol, headed by one of the engineers that opposed the launch to begin with. Starting in late 1986, they worked out of temporary quarters near the Morton Thiokol facility in Brigham City, Utah. First, they were instructed to come up with a solid rocket motor that was safe to fly. Second, they were to minimize the impact on the schedule to return to flight by using existing hardware to provide the engine, as long as it could be done without compromising safety. Work got underway and included a rigorous testing program that resulted in the decision to stay with the original O-ring material rather than introduce a substitute.

In late 1987, Wiley called me into his office. He asked me to sit down at the conference table, and then joined me. I could tell from how he was acting that he was about to ask me to do something out of the ordinary.

He looked right at me, stone serious. "I told NASA that we're going to put a representative for quality assurance on the team in Utah," he said. "I'm sending you to be the deputy lead on this team. I want to make sure they've looked at every possibility they can before they make a decision."

I smiled. "You know I don't know a thing about O-rings, Wiley."

"I'm not worried about that," he said matter-of-factly. "Just go do your job. Analyze, be critical of the processes, and use your strategic thinking to your utmost. Amanda, I need you to listen, lead, and learn."

*I can do that*, I thought. *That's what I've been doing ever since I came to Marshall, thanks to you.*

"Amanda, I need you to listen, lead, and learn."

Wiley continued. "You won't be there alone. Others from Marshall will be there. I'll be there from time to time. I just need you to help them make the right decision."

As I walked out of his office, my head was spinning. *This is huge*, I thought, *and Wiley picked me. Me. But I trust him. Honor him. I'm not going to let him down.*

I flew into Salt Lake City, then drove to the hotel in Ogden, Utah that was a little less than an hour away from Thiokol. The drive from the hotel to the facility was one this Alabama girl wasn't used to. I passed by salt flats, hot springs, and little else. It was barren and desolate. When I arrived and got ready to attend the first of what was going to be many long meetings to come,

Wiley, who was indeed there as he said he might be, pulled me aside.

"You know they don't want you in there," he said. "They think you don't know anything about what they're talking about. But I told them I don't care about that. They need to make you successful. And I've told them that's exactly what they will do."

He left to go inside, but I didn't immediately follow him. I needed to reflect. *That's a sponsor,* I thought to myself in appreciation. *He has my name engraved on his chest. He's doing right by me.* I also considered those in that room who didn't want me there and remembered my encounter with Jim. *You don't have me. You don't control me. Tell me I can't do something, and I will do it.*

*Be bold.*

And I was. That first visit to Thiokol lasted three weeks, and I returned three more times over the next three months. There were different sub-teams with different emphases, and I was the deputy on my sub-team that focused exclusively on the O-rings. By this time, decisions had been made to redesign the boosters so that the next O-rings chosen would work with a J-joint system that made it harder for gasses to escape around them if the O-rings failed. In addition, several types of O-rings had been chosen as the finalists for selection. In every meeting, we looked at those types, assessing data about them, scrutinizing the materials they were made from, and analyzing how they functioned when it was too cold or too hot. Each O-ring had a different footprint and varying degrees of performance.

We went on trips to visit the various O-ring vendors, meeting their staff and evaluating their work. We examined test data and design criteria and assessed the O-ring types according to that criteria. Time and again we tenaciously asked, "Did you think of this?" "Why did you do it that way?" "What kind of analysis did you do?" We questioned strategy as well as technical execution and did all we could to validate that what was being done was correct. It was a thorough but laborious process.

I did everything Wiley had allowed me to do before at Marshall and had prepared me to do now. Each session brought us ever closer to a solution, like a tortoise moving slowly but undeniably toward the finish line.

Our choice had to be right. What happened to Challenger must never happen again.

In the end, my sub-team voted and submitted our recommendation—and the O-ring was chosen and approved all the way to the top levels of NASA and Morton Thiokol. My sub-team's work was finished by early 1988. Later that year, on September 29, Space Shuttle Discovery launched, and NASA returned to flight. It had been almost three full years since the Challenger disaster.

I felt I had been part of something significant.

Historic.

I was making an impact as an engineer, growing as a leader, and I was in no hurry to slow anything down. I was Miss NASA—and I was on a roll that was about to take me on a Rocky Mountain high.

My sister Yolanda, who after graduating Tuskegee went to the University of Alabama law school and worked in the patent attorney's office there for a few years, had just taken a position at Marshall as an engineer in the shuttle program management office. We started visiting with each other at work when we could, though our professional duties never crossed paths. At the same time, I progressed through a series of promotions as a junior engineer that ultimately resulted in an assignment, on behalf of Marshall, to two different Lockheed Martin facilities and at Ball Aerospace in Colorado.

I arrived there in early 1989, got an apartment in Denver, and ended up staying there for a year-and-a-half. I served as a quality assurance resident manager and focused on satellites deployed by the shuttle. One satellite I worked on was tethered to the orbiter and extended far out and away from the vehicle into Earth's upper atmosphere to provide meteorological measurements. From a leadership aspect, it was more engaging than the earlier work I'd done on cargo bay elements and other projects at Marshall, but from a hands-on perspective it was less engaging because I couldn't touch anything being worked on.

Still, the Colorado opportunity was all part of Wiley's ongoing process to enrich, boost, and position me to someday qualify for his job at Marshall. It was an amazing experience professionally and an interesting one personally, especially living for a while in someplace so different from the deep south. I purchased a new car while I was there, a cute, red Nissan 300ZX with a T-top that was sporty, fast, and—as I found one day to my peril—slippery on a snowy road. I hit some black ice and did a half turn right in the center of a six-lane highway,

84

but thankfully no one hit me. I certainly never had anything like that happen in Alabama. There was a wind chill of sixty below zero on the day my assignment in Colorado came to an end. It was so cold it hurt just to breathe.

I welcomed the warm sun upon my return to Alabama and was promoted once again—to quality branch chief, the same level my supervisor held when I first arrived at Marshall fresh out of Tuskegee. My office was in the same building as Wiley's, downstairs and down the hall, but in the same building nonetheless. Best of all, I was given my first administrative assistant, my own team of quality assurance technicians and inspectors, a couple of engineers, and even a student aide. I was flying high! I wanted to become a leader and have influence over people, and here I was! I interacted with Wiley, who was still my mentor and sponsor, as well as with Inellia. In addition, I attended more meetings, including senior-level sessions that I'd never been to before. When I could, I still saw Yolanda as well, happy to again have her company.

My team and I worked on shuttle payloads, similar to previous ones but with some new elements such as crystal growth experiments and added components for the Hubble Space Telescope, which had been launched in April 1990. My team was independent and self-directed, and I was often needed to facilitate conversations with others in leadership or resolve conflicts my team had internally or with other entities at Marshall.

Over the next three years, I took on tasks of increasing importance, primarily as a leader of people. I worked on tiger teams, a group of experts in different fields who looked for the root cause of a specific problem with the tenacity of a tiger stalking her prey to come to a quick resolution. I led technical interchange meetings where we reviewed test data, analysis, and research to discuss how to better understand a difficult issue. It was like a brainstorming session on steroids. I shifted from working solely on payloads to other shuttle elements such as external tanks and engines, all with the goal of quality assurance. In light of what happened to Challenger, I engaged in each responsibility with renewed rigor and attention with the increased realization that more was at stake than successful shuttle missions. Lives hung in the balance of everything we did.

Lives hung in the balance of everything we did.

My engineering career was becoming all I hoped it could be. I was thriving at Marshall in February 1993 when Wiley called me on the phone. It was a Thursday afternoon.

Just the sound of his voice told me something was up.

"The space shuttle program is on stand down, Amanda," he said. "We're having turbo pump challenges on the main engines, and some of our people are needed to work on the issue. They're looking for someone to be a quality assurance resident manager."

I rolled my eyes. *What is he getting me into now?* I asked myself. I knew that I had attained a level of trust in Wiley that allowed me to believe he would never ask me to do anything that was going to harm me. He always placed me where I could succeed.

"I told them you would go," he continued, "so when they call, you better take it."

I was honored, as I usually was when Wiley advanced me forward, but I was also a little surprised at the impromptu nature of his decision. He was talking like I had a choice, but I understood that I really didn't. "Where do I need to go?"

"Los Angeles. Canoga Park."

*I don't want to go to California. But you did tell him you wanted his job. This goes with the territory. Still, I can't believe he just did this.*

We hung up—and I got the call the very next day. That's when I learned it was a rotational assignment, meaning I wasn't going to be on temporary duty there. L.A. was going to be my new home, at least for the next year and maybe longer. "When do you need me out there?"

"Sunday. That way you can start first thing Monday morning."

I gasped. "Sunday." My voice went up an octave. "You mean *this* Sunday?"

That was affirmed—and I started packing my bags and making the arrangements with NASA to move my belongings. I went with renewed determination.

*I'll go, do my job, but I'm not going to meet any people or make any friends.* The mindset was my way of declaring my independence, since in every other way I was being told what to do. *I'm just going there to work and nothing else.*

So off I went to la-la-land with no intention of seeing the sights, hitting the beach, or gazing at movie stars. I found an apartment and settled into my new job with exhaustive precision. As quality assurance resident manager, I led several teams that addressed the turbo pump issue as well as worked on all major components of the main engines: nozzle, coolant pipes, wiring and insulation, and the impellers and turbo pumps. Each component had its own quality person under my oversight, and I did regular walkabouts to make sure the various work areas were safe, that workers were wearing their personal protective equipment, and that every government-mandatory inspection point was where it needed to be for each component.

After a while, I did soften my "all work, no play" stance. I made some friends in Canoga Park and we attended concerts together at a bring-your-own-lunch outdoor park where I saw artists such as Stevie Wonder perform. I also found a church to attend on Sundays that several movie and TV stars also frequented, though I had to be told who most of them were. I still missed home, but la-la-land didn't end up being as bad as I thought it was going to be.

By the time a successful redesign of the turbo pumps was completed, the quality standards had been set at a higher level, and a no-fail culture was instilled. I put in to return to Marshall and ended up back in Alabama after just one year away. My time in Los Angeles was eye-opening for me as a leader. I discovered that I was sometimes too short in my communication with others and at times too harsh in how I wanted tasks completed. That was the overall NASA culture back then and I exemplified it, but that didn't mean it was right. I learned that I needed to listen to my team members more and not stretch and stress them too far. I also understood that I had to better leverage the diverse skills my team members brought to their roles, and I had to become more creative and innovative in encouraging them to do what needed to be done.

I was leading people, just as I'd always wanted—but realized I still had a lot to learn.

Upon my arrival at Marshall in September 1994, the temporary promotion I received to go to Los Angeles was made permanent. I became GS15 Director of Systems, Safety, and Reliability, but there was a big difference. Wiley was no longer there. During my time in Los Angeles, he had become ill and had to retire. Without his presence, my sponsor was gone, but he had equipped and prepared me so well that I knew I was ready to move forward without him. He had given me all the experience and exposure I needed. Now it was up to me to take it from there. Plus, I wasn't alone at all because Wiley's replacement was kind to me. It was a different relationship than I had with Wiley, but he was supportive, and I honored him as I did all my leaders. Not long after, Wiley passed away from lung cancer.

Making my new position even more challenging was the fact that I had no practical experience doing the safety and reliability tasks my teams were charged to achieve under my leadership. Our focus was hazards analysis on all the shuttle elements, including all payloads under Marshall's responsibility. We looked at fault trees that broke down every unit or system component, what could cause each one to fail, and how to offset those causes. The goal was to achieve 99.9 percent reliability on every shuttle system. Some components, such as wiring, had quadruple redundancy built in to ensure it was fail-safe.

Though I had never rolled up my sleeves and worked on these components before, my confidence was undeterred. My teams required a leader to facilitate, scrutinize, finalize, and approve every analysis they did. They needed someone to orchestrate and organize it all. That's what I felt I brought to the table. Using what I had learned in Los Angele as a guide, I encouraged everyone to be the best they could be and equipped them to expand their ability to see outside their area of expertise to discern how it related to other areas.

> I encouraged everyone to be the best they could be and equipped them to expand their ability.

My work was energizing and fulfilling—positioning me for an unanticipated, and even more fulfilling, change in my personal life.

I met Lonnie Goodson at Tuskegee, and we had stayed in touch intermittently since then, throughout my first, failed marriage and his own marriage that ended in divorce. We reconnected upon my return from Los Angeles as his divorce was finalized, intent on being friends and nothing more. He worked out of state, so we saw each other only on weekends, but Lonnie and I rarely missed an opportunity to get together. I'd always thought Lonnie was a nice guy, and I believed he thought I was nice, too, as well as a bit feisty because of my get-things-done demeanor.

As we saw each other more, our feelings toward one another unexpectedly progressed to the point that we decided to have a first "date." I had him over to my new house, acquired right after I returned from California, for dinner. I made lasagna (I make *good* lasagna), we sat at the kitchen table, and we talked. There was no candlelight, no mood music. We simply conversed—and as I told him about my goals, ambitions, and dreams, he resonated with what I was saying and even told me about his. This had never happened to me before, to be with a man with a receptive ear. I could tell that he really cared about what I was sharing and wasn't simply placating me to be kind.

But kind he was. Whenever he came over to the house, he did everything from replacing burned out light bulbs and dirty air filters to doing the dishes. He did all of this without being asked, just to be nice.

As my feelings for Lonnie began to grow, I gave him a list—I am an engineer, after all—of do's and don'ts. Included in the do's were items such as to treat me right, honor my goals and dreams, go to church, and believe in God. The don't list said not to yell at me, call me names, curse at me, hit me, or sneak around on me. That handsome, linebacker of a man read every one of them, then simply said, "Yeah, I can handle that."

I then had him date and sign the document. (Don't judge me. Some of you wish you'd had a list, don't you?)

He handed me the pen, and I looked at him. "Where's your list?"

"I don't have one," he said.

"You gotta be crazy," I retorted. "Everybody's got a list."

"No," he replied tenderly. "I'm just going to love you for who you are."

Meanwhile, I had become involved in a new church, Macedonia Cumberland Presbyterian Church in America in Decatur, where I had decided that I needed to get a bit more serious about my Christian faith. I got involved in more Bible studies and led a couple of teams at church. My pastor had also taken notice of Lonnie and must've seen what I didn't think anyone else could: that I was getting more serious about him, too.

She started asking me, "So, are you engaged?"

Each time I responded, "What do you mean?" I wanted to redirect the conversation.

She was undeterred. "You need to decide what he wants to do."

Time and again she questioned me, lovingly yet persistently, and it started to take root in my mind. I *did* need to find out where this was going. I wanted him to want me *totally*, and I needed to do what I thought was right in God's eyes. So, I had to know—even if I was a little reluctant to hear what he was going to say. I was concerned about being rejected.

On Thanksgiving, which that year also fell on my birthday, we were at my parent's home when I finally decided to find out.

"What are your intentions for us?"

It was as if I punched him right between the eyes. He looked at me like I was crazy. "I am just getting out of a serious relationship," he deferred.

"I know," I replied with a full-on, feisty tone. "But I need to know, or I got to go."

He was so surprised and upset by the unexpected confrontation that he turned on his heels and walked out, joining my father who was just leaving the house himself to go for a brief walk in the neighborhood. I guess I shouldn't have been shocked that he didn't reply right then, considering the pressure I was putting him under. Even after he returned, and we had our Thanksgiving dinner, he didn't respond. I settled in for a wait.

A couple weeks later during another weekend visit, I even went ahead and asked Lonnie to marry me—but he still didn't give me an answer. I knew I was coming on strong, but I truly felt I needed to know. Things were a little strained between us, but the friendship we had established up to then was strong enough to handle it. Plus, I sensed Lonnie was really thinking it through. I speculated that he was concerned that if we took the next step, we might lose the friendship we had and perhaps our entire relationship. It wasn't easy, but I remained patient and hopeful, trying to suppress any growing resentment at the delay.

Finally, at the end of January 1997, we were in Nashville together, and while we were out on the town, he popped the question.

I suppose I should've responded differently, considering the past several weeks, but I quipped petulantly, "I don't want to marry you. You didn't accept *my* proposal. You told me nope; I'm telling you nope." I was 70 percent joking, though I will admit I was upset because it had taken him so long. My emotions were a mess.

"But I mean it," he insisted. "Really." I could tell he was 100 percent serious, and not the least bit put off by the way I replied.

Still, I stuck to my guns. "I'll get back to you on that."

And I did—even if it was a few days later—by calling Lonnie and properly accepting his proposal. I was happy. I had a great guy who accepted me as I was and was going to love me without condition, and getting married was going to let me be right with God.

As expected, our engagement period was brief. We were married a few months later on May 24, 1997 at a ceremony inside my home. About fifty guests were there, family and friends including a handful of people from NASA. But I asked them to keep it a secret for as long as they could because by then I'd just been promoted again to SES Director of Safety and Mission Assurance—the *very* position Wiley held when I told him I wanted his job. The position included all the responsibilities he held, plus other key core areas of supervision. His faith in me and tireless willingness to give me opportunity had come to fruition.

I'd just been promoted again to SES Director of Safety and Mission Assurance—the *very* position Wiley held when I told him I wanted his job.

I had made it, but now that I had it, I didn't want to lose it because some higher-ups in NASA assumed I couldn't handle the position and be a wife at the same time.

I didn't have anything to worry about. The directorship was going to be mine for years to come—and some of my greatest challenges and surprises, as a leader and as a woman, were still ahead.

Chapter 6

# The Most Beautiful Thing

I didn't even realize I was going to have a baby until three months into the pregnancy. I'd never had a child before, so I truly had no clue other than feeling a bit more sluggish than usual. But when I did find out I was going to be a mother, Lonnie and I had been married less than a year, 1998 had just started, and I was cranking along at NASA.

By then, I had begun traveling to every shuttle launch. I oversaw internal, NASA-wide pre-flight reviews where every shuttle element and payload detail were discussed for risk and reliability. I attended flight readiness reviews in Florida involving my team usually led by the mission flight director. After each launch, we monitored retrieval of the solid rocket boosters from the ocean but didn't have any direct responsibilities for shuttle landings. I also traveled to NASA headquarters in Washington D.C. on a regular basis for key meetings connected to the shuttle program. My role there was to ensure that anything identified as a risk on any of the missions, especially regarding the safety of the propulsion systems, was mitigated, controlled, documented, and presented, as I participated in interchange meetings on safety, best practices, and NASA's evolving culture.

Finally, I began mentoring young engineers at Marshall, just as Wiley had done with me. I helped them to develop strategies to become better in their chosen areas of expertise and focus on goals to equip them to become what they wanted to be in the future.

Ironically, no one ever asked me to help them get *my* job. I guess my audacity with Wiley was unique.

I knew this relentless pace was going to continue unabated and wondered how being a wife and mother was going to fit into everything. But I was happy to be pregnant, even if at times I felt I had no idea what to do. Every day, I read portions of the book, *What to Expect When You're Expecting*, studying the craft of infant motherhood with an engineer's zeal and mindset. When the time came to attend childbirth classes, I went with my aunt since Lonnie still lived and worked away from home. It wasn't until I was seven months pregnant that he found the job at Daimler-Chrysler and was able to stay with me permanently. Interestingly, as the pregnancy progressed, I never really thought about what kind of a father Lonnie was going to be, or how we were going to work together as parents. I simply assumed he was going to do well and that we'd figure it out together—and we did!

When Jelonni was born in June 1998, I just held him and gazed at him in awe. He was utterly beautiful and had a little bitty cry. I marveled at how God had created something so amazing in me. I took eight weeks of maternity leave and in that time, I bonded with my baby son—and I also dove into motherhood with the same determination and rigor that I brought to my NASA duties. To be a good mom, I thought, I had to be attentive to every need, be there every moment. I hardly slept, in part because Jelonni was awake every few hours, but also because I felt I had to be awake and there for him. When Jelonni got colicky, Lonnie put us in the car and drove around in the wee hours of the night in hopes the motion would put Jelonni to sleep. We set him in his seat on top of the vibrating washing machine, walked him and rocked him, and did whatever we could to settle him down. I grabbed some sleep during the day whenever my aunt, parents, or Yolanda could take him. Lonnie was kind and sensitive throughout the leave, too, though his role was limited because he still had to be at work.

When my leave was over, I tried to find a balance between being a nurturing wife and mother at home and an effective, focused leader at work. I compartmentalized the roles like they were different rooms of a house: the utility room is for laundry, the kitchen is for cooking, the bedroom is for sleeping. So, work was for Amanda H. Goodson, Miss NASA; home was for Tammy, wife and mother. At the same time, my desire to progress professionally took a next step as I decided to pursue a doctorate degree. My motivation came in part from my father. He had retired by then and been diagnosed with cardiomyopathy, a disease that makes it hard for the heart to deliver blood to the rest of the body. He had started to weaken and lose weight but remained as spirited as ever about me and my future. He felt that if I was going to be coaching people at work and maintaining my leadership roles at church, I needed additional training to do it all from a biblical viewpoint.

I appreciated that, but frankly, I followed his advice just as much to get the title. I wanted to see "Dr." in front of my name. I began school to get a doctorate in church administration, figuring it was going to profit me not just in my NASA duties but also at church by helping me enable degreed people to interact and serve efficiently with others who hadn't completed high school.

My studies also had an unexpected benefit: I studied the Bible more and learned more about it than I ever had in my life. As I did, I thought, *This is pretty cool!* The characters I learned about from the Bible had such faith and a veracity for life, and they provided lessons I could immediately apply to what I already knew about leadership. I completed the doctorate in 2001—but my father never got to call me by the official title I so desired. He passed away in February 2000 from heart failure. In the years that followed, I often reflected gratefully about what he instilled in me in terms of my education and the development of my self-confidence. Today, I am an ongoing legacy of what he poured into me.

There were no less than 16 different shuttle launches from the time I took over Wiley's old job in 1997 until the dawn of the new millennium. There were exactly 16 more from then until the launch of Columbia in January 2003. Each one had its own set of goals and challenges, but three were particularly memorable.

STS-91 in June 1998 saw the final docking of Space Shuttle Discovery to the Mir Space Station. Over four days, more than 1,100 pounds of water, and almost 4,700 pounds of cargo experiments and supplies were exchanged between the spacecraft. The Alpha Magnetic Spectrometer, designed to look for dark and missing matter in the universe, flew for the first time on that mission. The launch countdown proceeded smoothly except for a slight delay in operations to load the external tank with cryogenic propellant to evaluate a few technical issues.

In July 1999, STS-93 had a problem just five seconds after liftoff when flight controllers noted a voltage drop on one of Space Shuttle Columbia's electrical buses. Because of this voltage drop, one of two redundant main engine controllers on two of the three engines shut down. The redundant controllers on those two engines, the center and right main engines, functioned normally, allowing them to fully support Columbia's climb to orbit. The problem was eventually traced to a hydrogen leak in the No. 3 main engine nozzle, caused when a liquid oxygen post pin came out of the primary injector during main engine ignition, rupturing three liquid hydrogen coolant tubes. The orbiter successfully deployed the Chandra X-ray Observatory, a telescope designed to detect X-ray emissions from hot regions of the universe, which my team and I had worked on at Marshall. STS-93 was also significant because it was the first shuttle mission to be commanded by a woman, Eileen Collins.

Finally, there was the launch of STS-103 in December 1999 where we worked through no less than nine delays and scrubs, some caused by mechanical issues and others due to the weather. When Discovery first reached the launch pad in early December, damaged wiring found in an umbilical between the orbiter and the external tank was detected for repair and testing. The mission was put on hold again after a dented main propulsion system line, which carries liquid hydrogen fuel for the shuttle main engines, was found during closeout inspections of Discovery's engine compartment. Yet another delay came when a routine inspection of the external tank's pressure lines revealed a suspect weld. To ensure that the proper welding materials and procedures were used, a thorough review of the process utilized during the fabrication of the lines was conducted.

Yet each challenge was faced and overcome. The crew of the Discovery conducted three spacewalks to restore the Hubble Space Telescope to working order and upgrade some of its systems so that it could begin its second scheduled decade of astronomical observations.

I worked long hours during those six years. But I also received some significant and humbling honors, including an Exceptional Service Commendation and Federal Employee Woman of the Year recognition. I also spoke often, traveling to places such as Georgia and Mississippi and sharing on subjects like personal warranty (doing what you say you are going to do) and technical careers in engineering, all serving to inform the public about the value and impact of the space shuttle program. It was rewarding work. I knew I was making a difference in the lives of those I interacted with and was influencing the establishment of a more accessible culture at

NASA. People said I was down-to-earth and easy to talk to, which I felt allowed me to demystify communication with NASA leadership.

I felt fortunate to have successfully woven a tapestry where all the strands of my life had come together in one place to culminate in me becoming the leader I wanted to be and felt God had created me to be. All the challenges I faced and overcame in my childhood and in college had prepared me for what I was doing.

By 2002, we had started seeing repeated instances of "popcorning" issues where insulation foam off the external fuel tank created little divots on the shuttle's belly and undersides of the wings during launches. It was just another aggravating issue that not only frustrated me and my team at Marshall but necessitated additional diligence and attention throughout NASA. As an agency, we had so many successful missions without a repeat of something as horrific as Challenger in 1986, but we didn't want to get comfortable. We couldn't. Space flight came with so many layers of complexity—but it seemed like by the time one problem was identified and solved, two more cropped up to take its place. It was a bear, but I felt every mission, and especially every launch, was on my watch. Nothing could go wrong, but that constant pressure of trying to anticipate for the unknown kept the heat on.

All the challenges
I faced and overcame
in my childhood and
in college had
prepared me for what
I was doing.

Yet it was not what was happening at work that was getting me more and more exhausted. It was everything I was doing at home, trying to be a superwoman wife and mother, that was wearing on me. I couldn't help it. I strived to do everything at peak efficiency because that's how I was wired. I refused to settle for anything less than my best, and my best was probably almost always more than was required. But I hadn't learned that yet. I also hadn't learned what true rest looked like. No one had ever modeled it to me, so while I took breaks and thought I was relaxing, I never really did.

Just as it was before every shuttle launch, my life was a "go." It was probably going to take something major, something life-altering, to break the cycle and change my life's path.

The Columbia disaster in February 2003 was my last space shuttle mission. The trauma that followed, and career change that summer that accompanied it, broke that cycle and changed my path forever. God set me on a journey that has given me a completely unexpected but wonderfully fulfilling platform to work today with leaders and entrepreneurs—even if it's genesis over the next four years was going to be through something I never could've anticipated and never thought I would've wanted.

When we arrived in Tucson, Arizona for my new role at the engineering company, Lonnie also took a position there as an engineer in operations. Similar to when Yolanda and I were at Marshall simultaneously, Lonnie and I didn't work in the same department and rarely saw one another during the workday. My family also had an extra addition to begin our stay in Tucson. Ashley, an 18-year-old girl that I had known since she was little, agreed to come with us and take care of Jelonni as a live-in support in return for her going to the University of Arizona to pursue a degree in engineering management. It was an ideal arrangement since both Lonnie and I had full-time jobs and it was important to us that Jelonni be taken care of by someone who was just like family. Ashley was an itty-bitty thing, weighing no more than a buck ten at best, but even as Jelonni got bigger she held her own with him and was invaluable to us. She went on to get her degree, get married, and start her own family. By then, of course, Jelonni was old enough to take care of himself even as Lonnie and I continued working.

The rest of 2003 saw three dynamics at play. The first, my family life, was distinctly positive. We initially lived in a big three-bedroom apartment which was memorable for my first encounter with one of the desert's most recognizable critters. In Alabama, we used rotating water sprinklers that made a familiar *ch-ch-ch* sound to soak our lush, green yards. Such sprinklers were rarely used in the dry, sand-and-cactus laden yards of most Tucson homes. But every time I walked up to my apartment door, I heard that same *ch-ch-ch* noise and had no idea what could be causing it—until I noticed the rattlesnake curled in the corner by the stairs. I was so grateful to her. I had been hearing its warning rattle! It was a good thing I never got close enough to test the snake's patience.

That added to my already apprehensive attitude about the other creatures I'd heard dwelled in the desert southwest: lizards, scorpions, and big, hairy tarantulas. But I quickly discovered that while such things are around, they generally stayed out of sight because they were as afraid of me as I was of them. That was a good thing—because my family and I started exploring our environment with zeal. We loved taking walks in the neighborhood and learning how lush, in its own way, the desert actually was, especially when all the succulents, bushes, and trees were in bloom. When we moved into a home a few months after our arrival, we had lemon, orange, and grape-fruit trees, and we made more fresh juice than we could ever drink. We only did the juicing by hand once, though, because while it was fun, it was also wrist-twisting work. The air was dry, something we had never experienced in humid Alabama, and we did tons of outdoor activities together.

And that's what was so positive—we did things as a family in a way we never had the time or opportunity to do when I was at NASA. Out west, away from our extended family members, all we had was each other. That was more than enough for us.

The second dynamic, my work life, wasn't so positive. I came to my new job assuming I was going to be a deputy to the person who oversaw mission assurance for the company; instead, I ended up being the mission assurance person on a specific piece of hardware. That was disappointing, and my adjustment was made harder by the fact that I was very much on my own. At NASA, I was the go-to person with teams of people working for me on a myriad of projects. At my new job, I had no team, and I had no sponsor like Wiley. The responsibility to make sure the

We did things as a family in a way we never had the time or opportunity to do when I was at NASA.

hardware was built to the specifications required, and to assess and decide what to do with any problems with the hardware, was mine alone. There was pressure to meet our customer's needs to build the hardware a certain way for a specific purpose. I was used to the NASA culture and now I struggled to adjust to the new company's culture. When I asked questions or sought help, a welcome practice at NASA, I was silenced or shut down at my new employer.

I wasn't used to that and started to believe, even speak, that I wasn't going to be successful. Later I repented of that with the understanding that I was undermining myself with my negative confession. But in the moment, it was difficult, and even something as mundane as my work area was problematic for me. I was given an office, but when I first arrived it was being remodeled and I was placed in a tiny cubicle, much smaller than my first workstation at Marshall. One afternoon, Lonnie came in and commented, "Look at Miss NASA being humbled." I looked him up and down and thought, *I know that didn't just come out of your mouth.*

But he was right. I was being humbled, and I was going to discover that I needed to be humbled, and for a specific purpose—because the third dynamic, the one that seemed equal parts positive and negative, was my spiritual life. God had called me to Tucson and to an entirely new way of living and working, but He didn't reveal why. I sensed there was more to it than just a new state and a new job but knew nothing more. Yet I couldn't help but feel I was being revectored by Him, prepared for something completely different. It made me uncomfortable and I didn't like that, but it also slowly made me more aware of His presence and purpose in my life, and that I did like, even if I didn't know exactly where it was heading.

As 2004 began, I was aware that the one-year anniversary of the Columbia accident was approaching, and my thoughts focused on everyone I knew who was still working on the shuttle program at Marshall. I hoped they were doing well. Looking back now, I was indeed genuinely concerned about them, but I also know I was still deflecting myself away from my own lasting trauma resulting from the accident. I had to keep my "not on my watch" mantra silenced and suppressed. In truth, I hadn't followed what was going on with the shuttle program since my departure from NASA. I was in a new city at a new employer trying to make a fresh start at a new life. On February 1, I saw news coverage recalling the accident, but that was about all I did that day other than go to church.

As I continued to adapt to my situation at the engineering company, Lonnie thrived in his role and even found his own Wiley, a sponsor who helped him progress in the organization. While I was frustrated for myself, I was happy for him, and despite his earlier quip about me being humbled, Lonnie was careful and sensitive not to talk about his successes in a way that could make me feel worse about my circumstances. In the meantime, I dove into church work as I never had before. We attended Phillips Chapel CME, a Christian Methodist Episcopal church. Because I had been ordained as a minister prior to leaving Alabama to provide the added credibility needed to my doctorate to allow me to officially serve in church settings, I was sometimes asked to be the speaker for services at Phillips. I didn't really see it as preaching, though I suppose that's what I was doing. I had no interest whatsoever in becoming a pastor.

I did lead a women's ministry through the church called "Never the Same" that ended up doing full conference and workshop events in Arizona, New Mexico, Texas, and Alabama. It was a non-profit organization dedicated to reaching women living in mid-sized cities such as Tucson and teaching them about leadership principles within the Christian church. I oversaw a team of ten people and we brought in keynote speakers and area talent to perform or lead worship. I loved the work. I also sang in the choir at Phillips Chapel and played the piano occasionally.

The next couple of years witnessed a transfer at work as well as a significant honor. I moved from mission to quality assurance, giving me an opportunity to once more manage people while working to make sure the hardware we were assigned met our standards and the requirements of our customers, mainly the United States Air Force. My level of satisfaction at work gradually improved and was aided when the company started also asking me to travel to represent the company as a speaker to our product and service vendors, and to employee resource groups. The honor came when I was recognized by the YWCA as one of their Tucson Women on the Move, given to those who were doing unique things to help the local community as well as in the workplace. One of my co-workers nominated me for the award without me knowing it. I was both surprised and affirmed by the recognition.

My supervisor at that time was Don, a former astronaut

and flight director at NASA who I had served during my time at the space agency. During one of my regular job performance reviews, we were reminiscing about our days at NASA and I felt compelled to bring up the Columbia accident and the ongoing challenges I was having in dealing with it. Knowing he had been there and done that, I asked, "How do you handle it?"

He leaned forward, elbows on his desk and hands folded in front of him. "Do you feel responsible for what happened?"

I again flashed back to my conversation with Rick Husband. "Yes. Even though I worked launches, it was still on my watch."

"Do you feel you and your team did the best you could?"

"I do."

He leaned forward. "There was nothing else you could've done to prevent what happened?"

"Not that I know of."

He grinned. "Then I have three words of advice."

*Here it is,* I thought excitedly. *Something I can use, something that'll help.*

"Get over it."

He didn't say it harshly or with any malice. He was quite matter-of-fact about it. His smile indicated his confidence in his statement.

"Thank you, Don," I said as genuinely as I could, and got up to return to my office. But inside I was lamenting, *That does me no good at all. What do you mean, 'Get over it?' It can't be that simple.*

And it wasn't—but over the next year-and-a-half, I encountered others who talked to me about grief and loss. Many of them had loved ones serving in the military who were grateful to me because of my role in what my employers did to support our Armed Forces. They helped me to see that soldiers and shuttle astronauts alike know the risks they are taking and accept the possible consequences. They're proud and honored to do it. Through the counsel of others, and with Don's blunt advice as the catalyst, I began to realize that I was taking the Columbia disaster personally and making it all about me. At last, I saw what I was really experiencing. It was trauma, yes, but it was specifically grief over the shuttle crew that was killed, and loss about my job transition from NASA.

Grief and loss. That simple, yet that complex.

Grief and loss. That simple, yet that complex.

That recognition allowed me to finally start the healing process, one that was stimulated by the Lord as He used me, even through my brokenness, to counsel and coach ladies through my work with "Never the Same." My pastor encouraged them to come to me instead of him for insights and biblical advice. I was equipped to offer both because of my growing love for studying the Bible and for prayer, and from how God was strengthening me spiritually through both. That had started, really, when I did my 40-day "time fast" before I left Alabama but had continued to develop since then and was now birthing a deeper relationship with Him and a softer approach to my leadership style. Through the opportunities to minister to others fostered at Phillips Chapel, and via my evolving capacities at work, I was learning to be more flexible and relatable as a leader, to listen more intently to my team members, and to allow them to be more independent thinkers.

By the time 2006 rolled around, I felt as settled in as ever at work and as engaged as ever spiritually at Phillips Chapel. I'd also begun some relationships at Trinity Temple CME, a sister church that we often visited as a congregation for church anniversaries and other special programs, including with Trinity's pastor, Leotis Barnett. He was a plain, unassuming individual, not charismatic or loud, and reminded me a lot of Lonnie in how humble he was. Pastor Barnett had diabetes and by the way I saw him eat I could tell he didn't pay as close attention to his health as he should've, but that was probably because being a pastor was everything to him. His health wasn't his priority. His church was.

Trinity, therefore, was a familiar part of my church life, and I had emceed a few shared events there between our churches— but it was still a shock when I had a very specific and telling dream about Trinity in July. It came right before I woke up at the usual time in the morning, and it was brief and undeniably vivid. I was looking out over the congregation, all bright and dressed in their Sunday best. I was standing behind the old, large, wooden pulpit on my left side of the platform. I could almost feel the grain of the wood through my fingers as my hands gripped each side of the lectern. I was leaning forward, as though I had just delivered some profound message to the people.

I woke up.

I sat up in the bed and looked over at Lonnie who remained sound asleep.

I couldn't see them, of course, but I knew my eyes were big as saucers.

*Why am I at Trinity? And why was I not at the other podium on the right side of the platform where laity read Scripture or announce the affirmation of faith, but behind the pulpit, the place where only the pastor speaks?*

It was odd. Strange. It made no sense. I attributed it to indigestion.

Then, two weeks later, I felt God tug on my heart again, just like He had back before we left Alabama. His message was simple. "You need to go to Trinity." I had no idea why, but it was clear: He apparently wanted me and my family to leave Phillips Chapel and start attending Trinity Temple.

I went to the pastor at Phillips and told Him what I believed God was leading me to do.

"No, sister," he said emphatically. "God is not telling you that."

I was relieved. "Good. I want to honor and respect you." I also knew as ordained clergy that I had to have his permission to leave Phillips, so I figured if God wanted him to know and me to leave, He'd tell him. Besides, I didn't really want to leave Phillips, anyway.

Then the Lord told me to ask the pastor again. I did, he responded the same way, and so it went, back and forth, three more times. God said do this, the pastor said do that.

Finally, the Lord said to me, "The pastor is going to release you. Today. Your destiny is going to be determined at 30th and Park." That's the nearest cross streets to Trinity.

I called the pastor—and he seemed to be expecting me.

"I'm glad you called. I've been talking to some other leadership in the church. If you feel that's what God is leading you to do, we want you to do that. Go ahead, sister!"

There it was, just like God had said.

"Okay," I responded. "I'll do it today."

I called Lonnie, who was out of town for some training, and told him what had happened. We made the switch as soon as he returned.

Our first service at Trinity was in August, and at the beginning, we were attendees only, though over time I was given the opportunity to read Scripture or lead prayers as part of the services. Trinity had all of seven people regularly attending Sunday services and had seen no less than five pastors come and go in recent years. I discerned that it needed stability and decided I was going to be loyal, fiercely so, to Pastor Barnett. I also felt led of the Lord to truly humble myself under his leadership, to do whatever he asked, and to champion him to others in the congregation.

When I started attending, the members of the church didn't mince words. "Why are you here?" "Who are you mad at?" They assumed I had to have some negative reason to be there, and they didn't want me and my family there to mess up their little group. It wasn't a good situation—but I knew the Lord had brought me there and I wasn't going to be moved. I quickly heard rumors of a takeover from two other attendees who wanted to remove Pastor Barnett entirely, but I'd have none of that. I was there to support him. That's what I believed was going to bring honor to God.

After a few months, Pastor Barnett asked me to fill in for

him a couple of times for Sunday service—in other words, to preach. I did it and never once thought back to my dream that was now actually coming to pass. As I saw it, I was simply fulfilling my mandate from God to support my pastor. If part of humbling myself under his leadership was to preach a service or two, so be it. I didn't think anything of it.

Then came the night of our monthly Bible study in December when I got a call from Pastor Barnett.

"I can't make it," he told me, his voice sounding strangely distant. "I'm not feeling well and am at the ER."

I told him I'd be right over, and Lonnie and I saw him at the hospital. They were working to regulate his blood sugar, and when I looked into his eyes, they didn't look right. He repeatedly asked for water. He also told us then that they were going to keep him overnight to lance a boil on his foot. We prayed with him then left, and I oversaw the Bible study that night.

The next day, Pastor Barnett almost died. During the procedure on his foot he apparently went into shock and had the first of what ended up being a series of strokes. I even understood that his heart stopped but that he was revived.

Pastor Barnett then went into a coma. It was the end of the year and I was on holiday vacation from work, so I visited him every day. I'd talk to him and tell him to wake up, that Trinity needed him. I prayed for him and spoke Scripture over him. But he remained unconscious.

Early in 2007, the CME bishop asked me to take over Sunday services at Trinity. Obediently, I preached every Sunday and protected the church from those who wanted to take over in the wake of Pastor Barnett's absence. I remained fiercely loyal to my pastor, just as God had directed me. And, yes, I finally did remember my dream from the previous summer. It was almost like a sense of deja vu. *Ah, so that's what that was,* I thought.

After seven months, Pastor Barnett finally woke up—but he was never the same again. After the combination of the strokes and coma, he never returned to his right mind. I'll never forget that day, though.

"G-g-g-g-Goodson?" he said, looking at me as I stood over his bed. "That you?"

"Yes, it is."

"Who's pastor at Trinity?"

I wasn't surprised that was his first question. The church was everything to him. I told him who it was because the change had been made a month earlier—but I don't believe the name ever registered in his mind. Had it done so, though, I think he would've been surprised.

I know I was.

I was appointed pastor of Trinity Temple CME in June 2007, doing the "most beautiful thing" the Lord had for me in the most unlikely way I could imagine. Over a decade later, I remained pastor and had seen the congregation grow to a core group of up to 50-65 people at peak times who have learned to praise and worship God more openly, love His Word, and give to the church and back to the community. I was still at the engineering company full-time, had launched a speaking and coaching service, and had become an independent, certified John Maxwell coach, teacher, and speaker.

I'd certainly come a long way from NASA and the traumas of dealing with the Columbia disaster, and an even longer way from my upbringing in Alabama. Young Amanda Harris had become Dr. Amanda H. Goodson and was indeed making an impact in ways I never thought possible. Along the way I learned a lot about myself, my faith, and my leadership—lessons that I'm convinced will help you transform your thinking, reignite your passion, and maximize your impact on the world around you as an astronomical leader.

Allow me to share those lessons with you.

I believe you'll never be the same.

Chapter 7

# Your Right Recipe

When Lonnie and I had our first date, you'll remember that I made him homemade lasagna. I did this because I wanted to please him, and I was confident my particular lasagna recipe was going to do the trick. Based on how much he ate that night (and the fact that we're still married today), I believe it worked like a charm.

The methodology used to make my lasagna was basic—and one that we follow in a variety of other ways every day. I started with a set of inputs: the correct quantities of meat, vegetables, seasonings, cheeses, and noodles. I then followed with the processes of cooking the meats and vegetables and seasoning them in a skillet, mixing the cheeses in a bowl, boiling the noodles in a pot and draining them in the colander, and then layering all the prepared ingredients properly in a pan. Finally, I put it in the oven to bake at just the right temperature for just the right amount of time. The result was an output: a hot, aromatic pan of tasty goodness.

Input. Process. Output.

It's basic, effective, and constantly in use:

At the ATM, we insert our card (input), the machine checks our pin number and account preferences to determine how much money we need and where to withdraw it from (process), and then it disburses the cash (output).

- At the washing machine, we drop in the dirty clothes and soap (input), determine the desired settings, close the door, and push the button so the machine can begin to wash the clothes (process), and then open the door and remove the mountain-fresh, clean clothes that are ready to dry (output).
- When we arrive at our home, we get out the key and put it in the lock (input), turn the key (process), and then open the unlocked door (output).

The Input-Process-Output (IPO) model has been around for a long time and is employed several ways. In business, it defines a manufacturing process that take raw materials as input, applies the manufacturing process, and produces manufactured goods as output. It is a widely-used approach in systems analysis and software engineering for describing the structure of an information processing program. In psychology, IPO has historically been the dominant approach to understanding and explaining team performance and continues to exert a strong influence on group research today.

It's no wonder, then, that I believe this process is essential in helping us to become effective leaders. You'll discover how it was at work throughout the story you just read about me, and you'll learn how it can be the foundational grid by which you can develop yourself and your teams to pursue excellence and flawless execution in all that you do in three domains—at work, at home, and in your spiritual life.

Here's how we'll break it down:

1. **Input** will *transform your thinking* as you identify your current reality's vision, mission, strategy, and goals for your personal life and how to align those to what you do as a leader professionally, domestically, and in your relationship with God.

2. **Process** will *reignite your passion* as you commit to develop your future reality to achieve outcomes that cause you to grow and mature as a leader over a long-term period and in all three domains.

3. **Output** will *maximize your impact* as you take what you have learned about your current and future reality to sustain the ongoing process—all while giving back to others and changing lives as an astronomical leader.

I believe you'll come to look upon it all as a recipe that you can trust to bring renewed flavor and sustenance to your life every time you call upon it. Of course, the recipe is only as good as the cook who is using it. Get the quantity of ingredients wrong, shortcut a step in the preparation, or try to take it out of the oven too early, and the result will be anything but savory.

So, put on your *toque blanche* (that's the fancy French name for a chef's hat), don your apron, and get ready to fill out your recipe card. By the time you're done, I promise you'll enjoy your meal time and again.

Just ask Lonnie.

## 1. INPUT: Transform your thinking

God has created certain creatures with amazing capabilities. The chameleon, for example, shows uncanny accuracy in nabbing bugs with its tongue. According to Matthias Ott and Frank Schaeffel of the University Eye Hospital in Tübingen, Germany, the lizards have eyes that work like the telephoto lens of a camera. That requires a positive and a negative lens. All other animals in the world have only a positive, convex lens. Theirs was the first discovery of a creature that also had a negative, concave lens. The two-lens combo gives the chameleon super vision.

### Vision

Being able to see in ways that others do not often makes the difference between success and failure. Vision is being able to see what cannot yet be seen, to picture in your mind something that you hope to bring to pass, a future that you aspire to achieve.

When I grew up in the shadow of the U.S. Space & Rocket Center in Huntsville, Alabama, I was near a place that displayed one of mankind's best examples of what was possible. I could go there and see spacecraft that had gone to the Moon and back, pretend to be an astronaut in simulated weightlessness, and imagine what it would be like to walk in space or even go to the limit of humanity's journeys and step on the surface of the Moon.

Back then, I couldn't possibly envision that I'd someday actually work *for* NASA and help our nation's space shuttle fleet go to and from Earth on a regular basis. But after I was hired by NASA straight out of Tuskegee, I did start to get a vision of what I could become: Director of Safety and Mission Assurance. I couldn't literally see me in Wiley's seat of authority, but I did picture it in my mind—and eventually made the audacious statement to Wiley that put the realization of the vision into motion.

Discovering your vision as a leader starts with imagining something you are passionate about doing in your **current reality** that will make an impact not only for yourself but address a felt need and bring value to others around you. What can you bring to light that will utterly change your life and your community in a way that will be noticeable? This may not be one thing at first, but several items. List them out and look for any commonalities. What themes emerge from your list that excite you? Narrow it down and see what comes out.

You might say, "Dr. Goodson, I don't know what I'm passionate about." But I believe you do know, you just haven't taken time to unearth it. This has been the case at first for many of my clients. So, after taking a look at their existing resume, bio, and website (if they have one) to see their current reality, I'll then coach them by starting with the questions, "What are the things you

What can you bring to light that will utterly change your life and your community in a way that will be noticeable?

are doing today that you like the most?" followed by, "What are the ones you least like to do?" The first question allows you to list what I call your "productive ways of being" to identify how you act and what you produce that adds value to others. The second question causes you to ascertain what I call your "non-value-added ways of being" by honestly evaluating areas where your attitude or actions do not add value to those around you. Perhaps you tend to get angry when you feel like your back is against the wall. Maybe you become controlling when your sense of security is threatened. These ways of being almost always stem from an area where your belief system has been challenged or violated.

As part of this process, I'll also ask my clients, "If I were to go to your stakeholders—those who know you well such as your spouse, parents, siblings, classmates, and co-workers—what will they say you do well or don't do well?" Hearing what others have noticed about you all your life can often reveal things you've never recognized in yourself. Perhaps you're naturally creative or maybe you are an encourager. It could be that you're great at organization or super at seeing the big picture. If I can, I'll briefly interview those stakeholders myself to get that answer. Lastly, I'll usually utilize a personality assessment of my clients such as DISC to discover these trends. Through this interview and evaluation process, I can get the information I need to help them find their passion and develop their vision.

Another key to helping my clients pinpoint their vision was revealed to me in the days immediately following the Challenger disaster as I went to work with my colleagues at looking at every system and variable that may have contributed to the accident. Even though the O-rings had already been identified as a prime culprit, we didn't allow that to deter us from looking intently at every other possibility. As I did this at work, while also pursuing my master's degree away from NASA, I began to see how much more I was motivated by standards, goals, strategies, and tactical execution than those around me. I didn't realize it then, but I was beginning to form a vision of how I was set apart—my distinctive—from those around me who were doing the same tasks. I began to identify the unique value I brought to the table to meet NASA's primary felt need at that moment: to find a cause for the Challenger disaster and implement solutions to ensure that it never happened again.

Pinpointing your distinctive is essential in finding your vision. I coached one person who was in a corporate management position but felt she didn't want to be there any longer. I asked her what she really wanted to do, and she mentioned interior decorating. She wanted to help others find the beauty in their homes so that they could design their interiors in a way that enhanced their enjoyment of living there. At the same time, though, she also mentioned that her colleagues often came to her for advice about challenges they were facing on the job or ideas on how they could advance in the organization. As she counseled them, she felt she was helping them see the beauty hidden in their own thinking that could help them creatively make their workplace and their responsibilities there more enjoyable.

I saw the distinctive right away. "Have you ever thought about the fact that you are an interior decorator of people's minds, a designer of thoughts that people can discover and use to help them move forward in life?" Her face lit up. Suddenly, she had a vision that she was passionate about that could not only make a positive impact for herself in her government contractor job, but also uniquely address a felt need and bring value to others around her at that job. Another woman I coached loved beauty products, stemming from her parent's ownership of a perfume making business. But she told me she also loved working with children and wanted to make a difference in their lives to bolster their self-esteem. What was the distinctive that emerged for her? She caught a vision for working with girls as a modeling coach and make-up artist as they competed in beauty pageants. It was something that brought together two different passions and allowed her to express them.

Once you have captured a vision, you should then write that out in a specific vision statement. I recommend starting this statement with, "I am to be the best..." which may seem audacious to some, but I want you to recognize yourself as the "best" at whatever it is you envision, as well as position others to see you as being the best at it. Then, once you have your statement in place, look at how you can apply it in the three life domains of work, home, and spirituality. If your vision can be applied at your current workplace, as was the case for me at NASA, find a way to speak that vision into action. My proclamation to Wiley that I wanted his job was what put that process into motion for me. If you discover your vision is not conducive to your job, begin to think about what must happen to bring life to your vision by transitioning from your existing job to a new one, perhaps even as an entrepreneur going out on your own. This may take time, but don't be discouraged. See the vision and act to make it happen.

At home, share your vision with your family and ask them to seek out personal visions for themselves. Just as you did for yourself, list all the responses and identify the commonalities. Then discuss together how you can work to make those visions a reality and how you can be both sounding boards and cheerleaders for one another. Done in an atmosphere of love, this can be a unifying process for your family. Finally, employ your faith by praying for your vision. Ask God to reveal the knowledge and provide the resources you need to make your vision happen. This is also when you can make sure your vision is in alignment with God's purposes for your life. Odds are, assuming He inspired the vision to begin with, you'll be amazed to discover how He will use your vision to bring glory to Him.

## Mission

Once you have discovered your vision and made your vision statement, you now come up with a current reality mission to support that vision. The vision sees what you are going to do; the mission defines what you are going to do.

In my Bible study book about the subject of missions, I identified specific aspects every mission contains. Missions are *impossible* by every reasonable standard because they are generally an endeavor that hasn't been done before. That doesn't mean, of course, that they can't be accomplished. Missions are *time bound* because the right resources must be available at a certain time to accomplish them. Missions are *time consuming* in that they will take more than a day or two to fulfill. Missions are not quick endeavors but require patience and tenacity. Missions are *big* because they are complex, requiring strategies and goals to execute, which we will explore later. Yet missions are *for everyone* because I am convinced each one of us was created for the times in which we live to do something large and significant. We are all part of something bigger than ourselves and have a purpose to pursue.

When I was being championed by Wiley at NASA, one of the many leadership lessons he gave me was to never bring a problem forward without already having thought through a potential solution for it. I listened, took notes, studied them, learned, and applied what I learned so that I got to the point where I could anticipate his questions even before he asked them and have ready, workable responses. When you develop your mission, you want to do the same thing. You'll consider and anticipate obstacles and problems that could challenge your mission and then come up with solutions to each one so that your mission statement is foolproof.

I use three primary methods to help my clients determine their mission: SPOT analysis, 360 analysis, and brainstorming.

Consider and anticipate obstacles and problems that could challenge your mission and then come up with solutions.

A *SPOT analysis* takes what we learned in our earlier discussion about "productive ways of being" and "non-value-added ways of being" to then look at your vision from the standpoint of four key tests of your current reality: strengths (S), potential areas for improvement (P), opportunities (O), and threats (T). Your strengths represent areas where you believe you are most effective and therefore place you in a position of advantage. Your potential areas for improvement can come from places where you feel you are at a disadvantage that therefore need more training or development. Opportunities constitute areas that you believe you can exploit to even greater advantage. Threats are elements, usually external, that can damage or even endanger your ability to fulfill your mission.

I encourage my clients to assess their strengths, potential areas for improvement, opportunities, and threats from any starting point with which they feel most comfortable. One of my clients, Adam, is the editor of this book. He chose to do his SPOT analysis using my "Goodson 9 Block," a visual aid that presents the following categories:

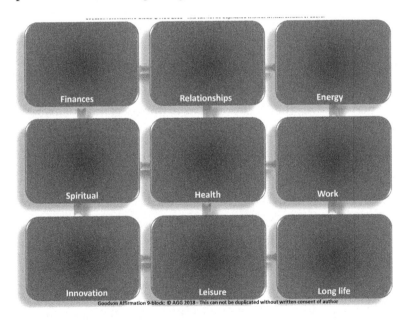

1. **F**inances
2. **R**elationships
3. **E**nergy
4. **S**pirituality

5. Health
6. Work
7. Innovation
8. Leisure
9. Long Life

Adam and I were able to discuss and list analysis points for each one. For example, in the Finances category, he was able to state that he was strong in tracking his income and expenses, but saw the possibility of using accounting software as a potential area of improvement that could create more time in his weekly schedule. He felt he could opportunistically exploit the knowledge gained from his tracking to pay for more strategic marketing to grow the income earned from his writing and publishing business. At the same time, he recognized that he still doesn't possess enough margin in his income earned to cover the threat of a large, unexpected expense. As he followed the same process through the remaining eight categories, we were able to reveal much of what he already knew about himself but had never articulated, much less scrutinized, previously. While it brought extraordinary details to light about each category, it only took about a half-hour—and rather than leaving him feeling overwhelmed, he was infused with renewed awareness about his business, his family, and himself that better positioned him to define his mission.

My Goodson 9 Block comes into play again later in the Process and Output steps as a tool to help you affirm and sustain your mission as it is executed long term. Notice, too, how the first letters of each characteristic spell out the term, "FRESH WILL." I love that, because your scrutinization of each one creates a fresh, renewed purpose to your life that gives you direction and propels you forward.

Next, a *360 analysis* takes the responses we received earlier from my client's stakeholders about what they do and don't do well and applies those answers to what the SPOT analysis has revealed. In Adam's case, he was benefitted and challenged to know what others had observed about his abilities in finances and other key categories. This feedback from those all around us—our significant personal relationships and professional peers—provides a full circle view vital to pinpointing a mission most likely to be successfully achieved. It helps us see our blind spots, bring them to light, and proactively address them. It also encourages us as we recognize the positive impact we have had on the lives of others.

Finally, *brainstorming*, by definition, means to produce an idea or a way to solve a problem by holding a spontaneous discussion—but as I work with my clients on their mission, we take it a step further by making it both more free-thinking and completely judgment free. The best brainstorming starts with open-ended questions and goes from there. We'll write down whatever answers come to mind. It can be something that seems crazy. Nothing is off-limits. We also want to make sure we're engaging the subconscious mind, which takes some time since scientists have learned that it takes a good 20 answers before we really start progressing from conscious thinking and into our subconscious.

We keep the process going by using brief, sound-bite-sized answers whenever possible and by not allowing ourselves to impose any discriminatory limitations on our responses. We move fairly quickly and once we feel we have all the possible replies to a given question, I'll ask clients to try and provide one more. It's like doing reps at the gym and once you're done on a certain machine the trainer asks you to do one more rep. Just like that pushes the body physically, my brainstorming process pushes the mind and builds your mental muscles. This can be challenging for some people depending on how analytical or creative they are, but the earlier SPOT- or 360-analysis steps usually keeps the client from going too far into one extreme or the other.

Once some or all of these processes are completed, we use them to identify your mission, confirm that it stems directly from your vision, and then develop a mission statement that clearly articulates what you wish to accomplish right now in your current reality. Once this statement is finalized, you are then able to address the three life domains of work, home, and spirituality in light of your mission.

At work, discover if your mission can feed into the organization's mission. At NASA, my mission to become a leader of people fit seamlessly with the organization's need for leaders who could do exactly that. If your mission doesn't fit with your current vocation, think about what it'll take to fulfill your mission apart from work. You may have to start a part-time job that slowly builds until it can create full-time income to allow you to transition from your employer. With your family, talk about how you can pursue your mission and either incorporate it with your family or do it while still maintaining your responsibilities to your home. It is best if your family gives their full buy-in and agrees to support your mission. Then, as you begin your mission, activate the tools of your faith to empower you to run after it with every fiber of your being. Spiritual disciplines are essential and will give you focus to support the execution of your mission.

## *Strategy*

With your vision and mission in place, you now need to develop a current reality strategy, a well-thought-out plan to fulfill your mission. Think of a blueprint for a building. On it, you will find details on how many rooms it will have, what those rooms will be used for, how big they will be, what features they will include to achieve each room's purpose, and how much each room will cost. It provides a visual representation of the building that a company can then use to construct the building according to exact specifications.

In the same way, your strategy will provide the blueprint for your mission, detailing each step required, in linear, chronological order, to make your mission happen. Each mission strategy will have several "how-to" steps, the amount of which will depend upon the complexity of your mission.

When I declared my mission to Wiley to someday have his job at NASA, one of the strategic steps I employed to fulfill that mission was to honor him as my leader. Every time Wiley fed me expertise and wisdom on leadership, I took that detail and utilized it with the goal of being able to think *like* him. Later, when I was serving NASA in Los Angeles, you'll recall that Wiley became ill and

Your strategy will provide the blueprint for your mission, detailing each step required, in linear, chronological order.

had to retire. I was given a new leader and I strived to honor him as I did Wiley. By then, I had also initiated other new strategic steps to support the accomplishment of my mission in response to several shortcomings I had identified in my own leadership style while in California. Four of those steps included working to listen to my team members more, learning to not stretch them and stress them too far, finding ways to better leverage the diversity of the skills they possessed, and becoming more creative and innovative in encouraging them to do what needed to be done.

Even going back to my childhood, I took strategic steps in support of my mission to interact with my schoolmates. By being calculating in how I took in what was happening around me, I was deploying a strategy of risk management—being part of the crowd yet not really *in* the crowd, protecting my uniqueness yet trying to use it to better fit in. Of course, back then I didn't know I was using a strategic step, or even that I had a mission. But that just shows that we often utilize strategic steps to achieve something even when we don't realize it.

You'll come up with the strategic steps for your mission by:

- Knowing what you want—Have a desire in mind and communicate it in a way that inspires you to action and makes sense to you.
- Making a mental note of your weekly process—Be an architect in your mind. Begin drawing the building by putting the foundational pieces in place, then adding the frame piece by piece and layer by layer in a logical manner.

- Writing it down and discussing it with an accountability partner—A trusted associate or business coach will help you see your mission and how to execute it in new ways, adding perspective and detail that may cause you to add a room or two.
- Rewarding your accomplishments fairly and regularly—Be your own number one fan and recognize your achievements in ways that are meaningful for you. One of my colleagues launched a stay-at-home business and promised himself that when he completed its fifth year of existence, he was going to buy himself a set of high-end, polo shirts with his company's logo on them. He saw it as a way to tangibly acknowledge his business's staying power. Today, he still proudly wears those shirts as he meets and works with his growing clientele.

When it comes to reconciling your strategic steps with the three life domains of work, home, and spirituality, there are two main factors to look at: competing and complimenting. In your workplace and your family, you have different individuals who are stakeholders. At work, these individuals can be your clients, coworkers, executive administrators, managers, and other leadership. If you are already in a leadership position, then your stakeholders are those you report to who impact your contribution to your performance. At home, they are your spouse, children, extended family members, or even your friends.

Once your strategy steps are set, you'll need to determine if any of them need to be realigned to not compete with, or to become complimentary to, your employer's or family's strategies to achieve their respective missions. You do this by a) knowing how you expect to move forward with your plan, b) asking for help often and early when you need it, c) requesting their support if there's a difference between what they think and what you think, so you can come to an agreement, d) finding accord on what you will and will not do, and what they will or will not do, and e) looking at the overall scope of the strategy's steps. How many hours will it take for you to achieve them, and what type of commitment will you need to maintain?

Not surprisingly, you follow the same evaluation process with your ultimate stakeholder, God. Spiritually, you want to make sure your strategy's steps don't disagree with and do honor the core tenets of your faith. In truth, there's no better way to affirm that your strategy is on target than to assess it with your core values in mind.

### Goals

There is a story that when the famed English architect, Sir Christopher Wren, was directing the building of St. Paul's Cathedral in London, some of the workers were interviewed by a journalist who asked them, "What are you doing here?"

The first said, "I'm cutting stone for three shillings a day."

The second replied, "I'm putting in ten hours a day on this job."

But the third responded, "I'm helping Sir Christopher Wren build the greatest cathedral in Great Britain for the glory of God."

That worker understood the vision, mission, and strategy that he was helping to make a reality and perceived the impact his contribution was having on his life and was going to have on the lives of others. Yet his role—as a mason—was to accomplish one of many goals Sir Christopher Wren had laid out to achieve the mission of creating the cathedral. It wasn't going to happen by chance. His vision birthed a mission that had strategies that needed goals to be fulfilled to execute the mission.

The problem with goals is that many people see them as nothing more than well-intended wishes. Think of New Year's resolutions. They are goals made in the fresh enthusiasm that often accompanies the advent of a new season, a second chance to do what we didn't finish the year before. But then, after a few weeks (or sometimes just a few days) they are once more set aside and left unrealized because the goals were not accompanied by disciplined action—or maybe because the goals weren't realistic to begin with.

You don't want that to be the case on your mission. The key to these inputs and to transforming your thinking is to correctly position yourself to *do* what you set out to do in your current reality. There's nothing like sustained success to morph your mindset and reshape your mentality about yourself and your

Setting the right kind of goals that are most likely to be attained for your strategy steps is essential to making your efforts prosper.

life. Setting the right kind of goals that are most likely to be attained for your strategy steps is essential to making your efforts prosper.

You've undoubtedly heard of the SMART Goals acronym—and for good reason: it works! Here's my take on each meaning and what can happen if you don't follow each one as you establish your goals.

- S = Specific: This means you have certain tests that you are going to do with your goals. They have a beginning and an end. They are clear to you. If you're not specific, you won't know when you get where you are going, can fall short of your abilities, can overshoot and do too much, or can overachieve on one thing when you should be working on something else.

- M = Measurable: This means your goals have mile markers along the way that confirm you are on task and going in the right direction. If you don't measure, you could end up all the way in New York when you meant to go to Chicago and need to backtrack. You need incremental steps to keep you motivated and on the right path.

- A = Achievable: This means your goals are within your sphere of influence or control. You can do them, and they are realistic. If they're not achievable, you can get frustrated along the way. Your goals may be too big or outside of your influence. It's like trying to go uphill on a skateboard instead of a Vespa.

- R = Results-focused: This means your goals are designed to show tangible results that are qualitative (it's characteristics) or quantitative (it's amount) so that you can prove you are accomplishing what you set out to do. If they're not results driven, you won't know how good or bad the goals were, how to change them to be better, or how much further you need to go to meet them.

- T = Time Bound: This means your goals will be achieved by a specific date or within a particular time frame. Without a deadline, you'll lack the discipline, structure, and order required to get them done.

Setting your goals using these precise parameters will often require you to come up with creative, strategic solutions— much like I learned to do in college through my involvement in the Institute of Electrical and Electronics Engineers and the National Society of Black Engineers. These organizations allowed me to be a champion and ambassador for the Tuskegee engineering department and gave me a chance to lead my fellow students to overcome the obstacles in the way of their goals. Just as those opportunities fed and nurtured my leadership expertise and capabilities, you will grow and mature as you do the hard but satisfying work of coming up with the right goals to execute your mission.

One of the most significant things you can do as we move through your current reality's vision, mission, strategy, and goals is to make a recording of our sessions and then listen to it daily over the course of each week. Your own voice is the most powerful affirmation you will ever hear. Every nerve in your body and every synapse of your brain responds because all of it is interconnected and programmed to recognize and heed what you declare. I believe this then energizes your spirit to make it happen. You can listen at home, on break at work, or when driving in the car. When I do this, I'll place jazz music in the background to infuse my creativity. I'll sometimes pray silently, asking God to bless and empower the very words I'm hearing. It's an incredible exercise.

Once your goals are set, you then need to evaluate them in light of your three life domains of work, home, and spirituality. In doing this, I like to think of Olympic swimmers who are confined to their individual swim lanes as they race one another. Each one of these domains is a lane of its own, yet they run parallel to one another and all reside in the same pool that is, in this case, the overall mission I wish to achieve. At work, I make sure that the steps I take to meet my strategy's goals can advance alongside my professional goals. I want to be viewed as an innovator and a person that is productive and creative while staying in alignment with the goals of my employer's strategy. At home, I assess my goals to ensure they don't conflict or hinder my family's goals and am careful to communicate to my loved ones the positive impact my goals have on them and on my roles at home. Spiritually, I bring to mind the Bible verse from 1 Corinthians 2:9 that reads, "What no eye has seen, what no ear has heard, and what no human mind has conceived — the things God has prepared for those who love him." This programs my heart and my intellect to engage my spirit so that I can progress, calling things that be not as though they were and seeing them come to pass (Romans 4:16-22).

We've seen how *input* will transform your thinking as you identify your current reality's vision, mission, strategy, and goals and how to align those to what you do as a leader professionally, domestically, and in your relationship with God. Now we will look at how mastery of the next step, *process,* will reignite your passion as you develop yourself to achieve the outcomes that will cause you to grow and mature as a leader—and move yourself to a different, higher, and greater place as you create, analyze, and enhance your **future reality**.

# Chapter 8

# Your Planned and Reimagined Future

During my personal development as a leader, I studied Tony Robbins, recognized as a world authority on leadership psychology and one of the top business and life strategists in the United States. He often talked about neurolinguistic programming (NLP), which according to Robert B. Dilts of NLP University encompasses "the three most influential components involved in producing human experience: neurology, language, and programming. The neurological system regulates how our bodies function, language determines how we interface and communicate with other people, and our programming determines the kinds of models of the world we create," he said, adding that "neurolinguistic programming describes the fundamental dynamics between mind (neuro) and language (linguistic) and how their interplay affects our body and behavior (programming)."

It's fascinating stuff—but simply put, NLP states that you can achieve the same results anyone else can if you follow the same steps and apply the same rigor and emotion.

In other words, when you stay faithful to the process.

We earlier looked at how process relates to following a recipe—but the fact is processes are all around us and are vital to successfully performing any task. For example, my editor, Adam, coaches his clients through six specific techniques for self-editing. It's a process he says any author of any book genre can apply to their writing to ensure the final draft of the manuscript will be as tidy and polished as possible. With his permission, here's what he teaches.

Step 1: Print it out. Reading your work away from the computer screen is essential. By moving your eyes from the monitor to the printed page, you'll see errors that you'd otherwise miss: misspellings, typos, spacing, and formatting among them.

Step 2: Read aloud and mark corrections. Using the printed version, next read it out loud. Don't whisper or read silently; by using your voice at its normal volume and hearing your writing, you will notice areas where the overall flow and rhythm is choppy and should be revised.

Step 3: Read silently backwards and mark corrections. This seems counterintuitive, but that's exactly why it works. You'll likely be shocked at the number of boo-boos and even missing words that you'll catch as you perform this step. It also makes your brain do something different from the norm.

Step 4: Proofread and mark corrections. Still using the printed version, you now perform an old-fashioned but never to be neglected proofreading run on your work, watching for punctuation, capitalization, and the like.

Step 5: Type in corrections and read aloud one paragraph at a time. Now you return to your computer, type in all your noted corrections to create your official second draft, and then read it aloud once more, stopping after each paragraph to type and fix any errors.

Step 6: Silently read electronically (the next day, if possible). Finally, you set the piece aside and then return, preferably a full day later, for one more silent read-through of the electronic version. There's nothing like reading it with a fresh mind and eyes.

See how it works? Process is an orderly, logical methodology that, when followed thoroughly, will make what you're doing better and successful. It allows you to have a quality output—and as a leader, the processes you follow, and how well you execute those processes, is essential.

## 2. PROCESS: Reignite your passion

With your current reality firmly in place, you are now positioned to do something I'm willing to bet you've never done before: select a specific point of time in the future, go there in the theater of your mind, and have a conversation—with yourself.

You might be thinking, "Okay, Amanda, hold on. What in the world would my past and future selves talk about? Sports? The economy? The latest Star Wars movie?"

You could gab about all those trivial things, I suppose. But I believe the most effective and enlightening conversation will come from your future self *revealing* to your past self what you have achieved, and then your past self *asking* your future self how you got there.

Can you imagine it? In this uniquely creative process, we will work together to have you dramatically determine your

> We will work together to have you dramatically determine your future reality before you get there.

**future reality** before you get there, seeing it as clearly as if you hitched a ride on a time machine, then travel backwards to your current reality by systematically, year-by-year, mapping out what you did do/will do to accomplish that future reality.

I can't think of anything that will reignite your passion more—and keep it burning—than deciding your own destiny! Let's get started.

## Back to the past

In the 1985 movie *Back to the Future*, teenager Marty McFly is sent back to 1955 to make sure his parents-to-be fall in love. If he fails, he'll cease to exist. If he succeeds, he can then get back into Dr. Emmet Brown's DeLorean time-traveling vehicle and return to his "current" life. Marty had to travel backward in time first before he could go forward and get back to his future.

In my process, clients do the same thing with me, but the opposite way. We'll first travel forward to a year in the future before returning back to the past and to your current life. Plus, instead of making sure previous events stay intact, you'll be determining future events, speaking them into existence as though they already were, so that you can then plan how to get there.

When I met with Adam to first discuss and complete his current reality, I spread a large sheet of butcher paper across two long tables. On the far-left end, we wrote down his vision, mission, strategy, and goals. We also placed everything we revealed about his productive ways of being and non-value-added ways of being, as well as what we discovered in his SPOT analysis, 360 analysis, and brainstorming using the Goodson 9 Block on the paper. Then I had him and his most important stakeholder, his wife and business assistant, move to the opposite end of the room. There, seated at the far-right end of the table, I then asked Adam to "become" his future self 10 years into the future. Notice I didn't direct him to pretend. I wanted him to be as present as possible while being his future self. Brow furrowed, Adam struggled with this exercise at first. Most of my clients do. But I eased him onward, telling him to revisit each Goodson 9 Block category and state where he is *now*, 10 years later, with each one.

This took longer than the half-hour we needed for the first Goodson 9 Block discussion, but with each revelation to himself of what he achieved in the future, he got more excited. He took ownership of each accomplishment, even if they seemed different and far greater than he thought they would be. For example, he declared an initial annual income goal that, I imagine, sounded generous to him. But, knowing what I did about him and what he had already achieved with his writing and editing business, I suggested a much higher income goal.

"Is that too much?" I asked.

I watched the gears grinding away in his mind as he took the dollar figure and made it real to himself.

"No," he said, "let's put it down there and then work backward to see if it's too much."

As he wrote the monetary figure on the butcher paper, I smiled—because I knew he was getting the idea. As we kept going, he made other business goals for himself and his clients, many of which he would've never considered had he not been 10 years into the future. Knowing he was going to have a full decade to accomplish the goals made them more achievable. We brainstormed innovations he was going to introduce that bled over into new services to maintain and expand his client base. When we looked again at the categories of energy, spirituality, and health, he set targets that were going to increase his vitality, grow his faith, and protect his physical and mental well-being. With relationships, leisure, and long life, I helped Adam identify a variety of travel goals to create opportunities to make ongoing, irreplaceable memories with his wife, daughters, and grandchildren, all of which happened because his income had increased so dramatically while his time spent working his business had decreased. Instead of working more for his money, we identified strategies he had achieved that had more of his money working for him. In the process, he organically addressed all three of the key life domains—work, home, and spirituality.

It was remarkable. By the time we were done using the Goodson 9 Block and another SPOT analysis to assess what we developed, Adam was ready to write a letter to himself that stated what he had accomplished in the future and provided an updated vision and mission for his business. Even more, his ability as a leader was infused because he suddenly saw himself able to achieve everything in that letter. His passion for his business and his life was reignited.

But we were just beginning. As he had prophesied in his earlier response to me, it was now time to work backward on each goal to come up with the strategies to meet them.

### Reverse planning through GAP analysis

When most people try to plan for the future, it seems daunting—and why not? It's like they're looking up from the bottom of a tall staircase. The first few steps may look easy enough, but as they consider how long the climb is, and the strength it's going to take to get to the top, they start wearing out even before they start. *Why should I make all these plans*, they think, *when I know I'm not going to make it all the way anyway? What's the point?*

That's why I never have my clients plan their future from the beginning, the present. We do it instead in reverse, from the end, the future, the top of the staircase. Looking down from the very pinnacle of their achievements, their mindset is completely changed. They don't see a climb, but a descent—a journey downward that, by the time they get to the floor, will have every step filled in with realistic, doable strategies that they've already seen and planned in advance from finish to start!

Adam, already a fan of strategic planning processes, enthusiastically understood. "I need to break down, by each year and maybe by each quarter, what I need to do progressively, step-by-step, to reach my goals," he said. Then he looked me in the eye. "But none of this will happen without the plan—and I need to work the plan. Whatever changes that plan demands, I need to face them with a positive attitude, and I need to be fearless and bold. I've learned that being fearless and bold has good results. When I set myself to do something, I generally get it done."

Then he added, his eyes wide and glowing, "Honestly, this whole process is revelatory to me. I'm not scared about anything I said about my future self. Back when I started my business it would have frightened me, but I've progressed enough now in my business and in my personal life to where those things hold no fear. I have nothing to lose and everything to gain. I'm willing to do whatever it takes to get there. That's pretty cool."

It *was* cool—and it will be for you, too, as you discover that you can achieve outcomes that cause you to grow and mature as a leader over a long-term period and in all three domains through reverse planning and by using the technique of GAP analysis. A tried and true tool, businesses use this analysis to determine what steps need to be taken in order to move from its current state to its desired, future state. It usually consists of 1) listing characteristic factors (such as competencies and performance levels) of the present situation or "what is," 2) listing factors needed to achieve future objectives or "what should be," and then 3) highlighting the gaps that exist between the two and need to be filled.

You can achieve outcomes that cause you to grow and mature as a leader over a long-term period.

My distinctive is in how I use GAP analysis (in reverse) and in who I use it for (individuals instead of businesses). To better understand reverse planning, think of how a GPS works. When I enter the address of my destination into the system, the GPS works backward to find the most direct route to where I want to go. It starts at the end point and progresses back toward the starting point. In doing so, it analyzes the trip by identifying obstacles along the way such as road construction or closures, estimating how long it'll take to get there depending on how much traffic might exist, and coming up with a street-by-street path I can follow and rely upon to complete the trip successfully. Then, as a result of its reverse planning, I drive onward to move forward toward my destination.

It's true that hindsight is always 20/20. If you have already been there, then you will know the steps to get there. That's one of the things that makes reverse planning so powerful and effective. As Adam started to latch on to this process, he said, "I like the idea of going backward because it forces me to think differently. What I am doing—now, 10 years in the future—*is* my reality and I am working toward that by going in reverse."

I then used my GPS example to explain another benefit of doing the GAP analysis in reverse. As I'm driving, sometimes something will come up that'll force me to deviate from the path the GPS planned out for me. It might be something necessary, such as when I receive a phone call mid-route which adds a quick errand for my husband. It could be accidental, such as not being able to merge safely over from the left lane when I needed to turn right, forcing me to backtrack. It may be as simple as a spur-of-the-moment choice to take another road for part of the journey because I liked the view it provided. Whatever it was, the GPS recalibrated to get me back on the correct route and keep me there.

In the same way, I told Adam, you will have some detours along the way. For example, a new financial challenge might come up in year four that could force him to alter that higher income goal we set for the future, or an opportunity could emerge in year six that would allow him to increase the end amount. The beauty of reverse planning is that it is flexible. It is revisited and adjusted on a quarterly, monthly, even weekly basis, but always in such a way as to keep you headed in the right direction toward the manifestation of your future reality.

With that perspective in mind, Adam and I set to work, looking at all of those goals we set from the nine "FRESH WILL" characteristics of the Goodson 9 Block. We determined what each one looked like going backward from year ten, to year nine, then eight, then seven, and so on, all the way to the year one. We started with Finances and the final annual income goal and did basic math starting from what he was making in 10 years and decreasing it incrementally to what he is making in the present day. Adam was encouraged to see that each yearly income increase was aggressive but doable. It was especially plausible when taking into consideration new income streams he had added via new services to maintain and expand his client base, as well as through other investments strategized with a certified financial planner to create a vibrant wealth management profile. Finally, we added in where Adam had donated portions of his income.

He identified organizations he supported and individuals he seeded into to support their endeavors. In all, about 10 percent of his earnings were used in this way, with another 10 percent set aside for saving and investing. We talked about how to leverage and move money so that currency was his friend, not something he was always chasing. I've always said of money, "You don't run after it. It should run after you." To assist with all this, the selection and hiring of a financial planner was placed in year one.

We ended with Long Life, which was where Adam chose to place his travel goals. He and his wife selected destinations they had visited as a couple and laid them into the plan: a getaway to the Italian Riviera in year five and a trip to Ireland in year seven. In year one, we started with the acquisition of passports. It was in year three that they had begun traveling with their grandsons starting with Legoland in California. They added trips with their youngest daughter, a professional jazz musician, as she performed across the country, and for their oldest daughter, a huge baseball fan, accompanying Adam to a new ballpark nationwide each year to see a game together.

In between, all of the other "FRESH WILL" components were planned, *as though they had already happened*, to fill out the gap between year 10 and year one. This took a couple of sessions and involved a lot more brow furrowing on Adam's part—but in the end he had it set out before him. It represented a detailed contract to himself of what he had done and when, positioning him to then add in the strategy steps and goals used to achieve each objective of his overall mission born out of the vision he birthed by determining his future reality.

## Enhancing and visualizing

After we have finished this first draft via the reverse planning process, I then work with my clients to enhance and improve our initial conclusions. We do this by examining each strategy and goal, year-by-year, to reveal any areas that need to be readjusted. I'll have my clients ask themselves, "Can I do this?" "What do I need to do differently?" Sometimes this is done by going forward on the timeline. Other times, we'll look backward. There's no hard rule. The point is to see anything that, for whatever reason, is inaccurate or simply won't work. This serves to "close" the gaps in the GAP analysis we completed earlier.

As Adam looked at some of the new services he pinpointed that made money for themselves, he determined that his year five goal to launch an online writer coaching curriculum needed to be moved a little later to give him more time to come up with the content to inform that curriculum. That forced him to reevaluate his income-earning strategies in that time period to ensure he had enough projected book editing or ghostwriting clients. Those were needed to make up for the funds that were not going to be realized as quickly from the online curriculum and still keep him on target for the income goals for those years. He then revised the other key steps connected to the development of the curriculum, from the writing of the initial concept paper, to research and consultation with other colleagues using their own curriculums, to the technical development, testing, and reworking of the platform tools used in the curriculum.

This, too, took some time, but Adam did most of this on his own, and then we came back together to review and allow me to provide feedback. Other clients have asked me to walk through this stage with them and be fully involved in each evaluation. Either way, we collaborate, and I'm helping you consider options you may have never seen before. Once each goal and strategy is revectored and finalized, we'll then take each set of yearly strategies and break them down into monthly objectives. We confirm that each one is specific, measurable, achievable, results-focused, and time bound. I like to use affirmative language: "I will do *this* by *this time*." That way, you know what you need to do by when—and you tell yourself you are going to get it done.

Adam and I then took my chart of the Goodson 9 Block and added images to it to provide a visual representation of the contract he had made with himself. Our minds process ideas using vivid, color pictures, and these images reminded Adam of the manifestation of his future reality's vision. Placed alongside these images were "I am…" statements that express the goal being realized in the present tense. I encourage my clients to create an electronic file of the chart and look at it every week, as well as to print it out and place it where they'll see it often, such as on the refrigerator at home or the bulletin board at the office. It's a simple but tangible way to keep that future reality "real" and forefront in their thinking. Adam often tells me how he sees the shot of Portofino, one of the towns of the Italian Riviera, and envisions him and his wife walking hand-in-hand on one of the narrow streets winding through the pastel-colored houses and small cobbled square which overlooks the harbor and the big, blue Mediterranean beyond the tranquil shores. Next to the photo is the statement,

"I am in the Italian Riviera with my wife, basking in the sun!" It's written as though it is happening right at that moment.

At that stage, we begin working the plan month-by-month—and as we do, we continue enhancing our initial conclusions through regular, ongoing coaching sessions. The process is iterative. With Adam, we start every meeting by looking at each "FRESH WILL" characteristic of the Goodson 9 Block. I'll ask, "How are you doing on each one?" We'll recognize and applaud progress while analyzing any setbacks and discussing solutions. I serve as a combination coach / consultant / mentor / cheerleader. During this time, I'm doing whatever I can to help you test, measure, and improve every goal and objective while ensuring each one stays true to your future reality's vision and mission.

### Your astronomical declaration

Think back to what we learned about neurolinguistic programming. I am absolutely convinced that what we think and what we say dictates what we do.

It certainly did for T. Keith Glennan, the very first administrator of NASA. He originally had the idea of landing a man on the Moon in 1958. But back then, his thought wasn't supported by reality. The political winds were not blowing his way. President Dwight D. Eisenhower was not a fan of space flight. He only halfheartedly supported it because of the challenges posed by the Soviet Union in its advancement of space technology. In addition, when NASA began, discussions centered only on getting a man into Earth's orbit, and the costs just to achieve that were astronomical (pun intended). Yet those realities didn't prevent the thought of landing a man on the Moon from occurring because visible circumstances are inconsequential to the vision of an idea for a mission.

So, Glennan devised a plan—with the help of noted spacecraft mechanical engineer Maxime Faget and other key engineers at NASA—to accomplish his desired future reality. But he lacked an essential ingredient to give the mission wings: a declaration. Glennan needed someone with authority to officially proclaim the mission. A proposed Moon landing had to have the enthusiastic support of the President of the United States. Such a declaration was required to marshal the resources of the federal government, without which the mission could not have any chance of success. As we know, that declaration was made by President Kennedy to Congress on May 25, 1961. "First, I believe that this nation should commit itself to achieving the goal, before this decade is out, of landing a man on the Moon and returning him safely to the Earth," he said. "No single space project in this period will be more impressive to mankind, or more important for the long-range exploration of space; and none will be so difficult or expensive to accomplish."

Incredibly, Neil Armstrong took his famous "one small step for man, one giant leap for mankind" a mere eight years later. Only 12 years after that, the first Space Shuttle launch took place. That event helped set the stage for my astonishing future reality that I have joyfully shared with you in this book, and hope to continue living, as I come alongside you to help you shoot for the stars as a leader.

My process to take you from your current reality to your

future reality reignites your passion so that you can make a declaration to live out your "FRESH WILL" and manifest outputs that bring your future reality to fruition. You can go to the Moon and beyond as an astronomical leader!

But the continued achievement of these outputs require two essential building blocks. With them, you will ensure your future reality truly *becomes* reality.

# Chapter 9

# Your Sustainability and Community

When New York City's Citigroup Center tower was first completed, it was the seventh tallest building in the world. Many hailed the tower for its technical elegance and singular grace, notable for its sleek aluminum sides and provocative slash-topped design. The structural engineer who designed the steel superstructure was William LeMessurier, who not long after the building was completed was elected into the National Academy of Engineering, the highest honor his profession bestows.

But according to Joe Morgenstern in *The New Yorker*, one year after the building opened, LeMessurier came to a frightening realization. The tower was flawed. Without LeMessurier's approval, during construction the joints in the structure had been bolted, which is a common and acceptable practice but does not make for as strong a joint as welding does. What made that a critical problem, though, was that in

LeMessurier's calculations he had not taken into account the extra force of non-perpendicular crosswinds. He concluded that the joint most vulnerable to such winds was on the thirteenth floor. If that joint gave way, the whole building could come tumbling down. He talked with meteorologists and found that a wind strong enough to buckle that crucial joint occurred every 16 years in New York.

LeMessurier weighed his options. If he blew the whistle on himself, he faced lawsuits, possible bankruptcy, and professional disgrace. He even gave a fleeting thought to suicide but dismissed that as the coward's way out. He could keep silent and hope for the best, but he knew lives were at stake.

So LeMessurier did what he had to do. He informed all concerned. City and corporate leaders faced the problem in a professional manner, and plans were drawn to strengthen the joint by welding steel plates to them. Contingency plans were made to ensure people's safety during the work, and the welding began. After the work was completed three months later, the building was strong enough to withstand a storm of the severity that hits New York only once every 700 years. It became and remains one of the safest structures ever built.

The repairs cost millions of dollars. Nevertheless, LeMessurier's career and reputation were not destroyed—but enhanced. One engineer commended LeMessurier for being a man who had the courage to say, "I got a problem; I made the problem; let's fix the problem."

You may come to a point as a leader where you realize your planned future reality has elements like that flawed building. By all appearances your strategies and goals look strong and poised to succeed, but you recognize there are points of weakness that make your entire plan vulnerable to collapse.

That's okay—because you can respond to those situations through the first of the two vital building blocks that allow you to take what you have learned about your current and future reality. Using those building blocks, you can sustain the ongoing process while giving back to others at the workplace, in your family, and in your spiritual fellowship.

## 3. OUTPUT: Maximize your impact

Sustainability is supported by a foundation of accountability. Just as LeMessurier held himself accountable to the potentially fatal flaw he discovered about the Citigroup Center tower, we will work together to hold you accountable to your future reality and its fulfillment. Yet it won't be through my input in our regular sessions alone that this will be achieved. I will help you find and utilize other key accountability partners in your life who will equip and encourage you to stay on course in every characteristic of the "FRESH WILL" Goodson 9 Block.

Who do you know that can fill these roles for you?

1. Finances: financial planner, wealth management coach, or CPA.
2. Relationships: counselor, pastor, or rabbi/priest.
3. Energy: personal trainer, exercise buddy, or body/ mind/performance coach.
4. Spirituality: Bible study partner, prayer/meditation coach, or spouse.
5. Health: nutritionist, therapist, or wellness coach.

6. Work: supervisor, human resources professional, or mentor.

7. Innovation: entrepreneur coach, mastermind group leader, or colleague.

8. Leisure: friend, spouse, children/grandchildren, or rest and renewal coach.

9. Long Life: travel advisor, life coach, or psychologist.

Each one of these people help you sustain your "FRESH WILL" through the accountability they bring and your positive, proactive, and integrity-driven reaction to their insights. For example, Adam has had high blood pressure for nearly 20 years and a few years back was diagnosed as being pre-diabetic. How did he respond? He hired a nutritionist to assess what he was eating and train him to make food-buying decisions and dietary choices that eliminated his unbalanced sugar diagnosis in less than six months. Adam was told he had a problem, recognized how he had caused the problem, and immediately went to work to fix the problem by being accountable to another person. Poor health was going to endanger his personal and professional future reality. He didn't accept that and did something about it.

As you achieve and maintain accountability for your future reality, I also encourage you to reward your success. The best rewards are those things that you value the most but are not going to undermine any of your other strategies and goals. For example, if you have a health issue like Adam, a big ice cream cone or a plate of cookies are inappropriate rewards. Instead, he bought some novels he wanted and gave himself extra reading time. Why? He highly valued the experience of diving into another world through a great story. Whatever those things are for you, create meaningful rewards to motivate your accountability.

As you work on being accountable, be sure to regularly evaluate your progress, and receive fresh feedback from your accountability partners. This can be done on a quarterly, monthly, or even weekly basis depending on what you are addressing. The new responses or constructive criticism and controlled praise that you receive from those holding you accountable will keep you on your toes, offset complacency, and keep you moving forward toward improvement or a resolution. Together, you'll come up with specific things to work on until you meet next, and you'll find yourself becoming more focused and self-disciplined.

As you achieve and maintain accountability for your future reality, I also encourage you to reward your success.

This output of accountability to feed your sustainability is entirely scalable and tailorable to your situation now as well as to what it will be three months from now or three years later. It makes you as fluid as your future reality plan has to be to succeed. It ensures you don't make it so hard that you can't achieve it, or too easy that it doesn't engage you and you end up not doing it at all. It creates momentum and decreases stress by increasing your capacity so that the plan doesn't overwhelm you.

Finally, it positions you to have the second essential building block to your ongoing output.

### You're not to be alone

Years ago, as scientists used the orbiting Hubble Space Telescope to peer at a cluster of some 2,500 galaxies called Virgo, they saw for the first time heavenly bodies that had been only theorized before: lone stars without a galaxy to call home. These isolated stars had drifted more than 300,000 light years, three times the diameter of the Milky Way, from the nearest galaxy.

"Somewhere along the way," John Noble Wilford wrote in *The New York Times*, "they wandered off or were tossed out of the galaxy of their birth, out into the cold, dark emptiness of intergalactic space." He added, "Astronomers theorize that these isolated stars were displaced from their home galaxies as a result of galactic mergers or tidal forces from nearby galaxies. There they drifted free of the gravitational influence of any single galaxy."

Like these isolated, wandering stars, you can drift from community. But you were never created for the cold of isolation. I believe God created us to be together in deep devotion to one another. He made us for the warmth of fellowship.

He designed us to live in community.

To live in community with one another is a must for the output of your future reality. Not surprisingly, it also significantly benefits your individual well-being. *The Journal of the American Medical Association* reported, "Building on a dozen studies correlating friendship and fellowship with health, a new study has found that people with a broad array of social ties are significantly less likely to catch colds than those with sparse social networks." The story continued, "The incidence of infection among people who knew many different kinds of people was nearly half that among those who were relatively isolated. The lack of diverse social contacts was the strongest of the risk factors examined, including smoking, low Vitamin C intake, and stress."

The same was shown to be true for those with more severe illness such as heart disease. In one study, Dr. Redford Williams, director of the behavioral medicine research center at Duke University Medical Center, "found that heart disease patients with few social ties are six times as likely to die within six months as those with many relatives, friends, and acquaintances." In addition, one of the main beneficiaries of being in community with others is our immune system. Dr. Janice Kiecolt-Glaser, director of health psychology at the Ohio State University College of Medicine, and her husband, Dr. Ronald Glaser, a virologist at Ohio State, reported "that a person's immune response to vaccines increases with the strength of his or her social support."

Where do you find such communities? Again, let's look at our "FRESH WILL" characteristics.

1. Finances: debt or financial education support groups.
2. Relationships: gatherings of friends or other married couples.
3. Energy: gym team or motivational group.
4. Spirituality: women's or men's group at church.
5. Health: friends who share your health needs or wellness support groups.
6. Work: colleagues or specific task focus groups.
7. Innovation: entrepreneurship or mastermind groups.
8. Leisure: friends who encourage or accompany you to rest or relax.
9. Long Life: 12-step support groups or travel groups.

Ideally, most if not all of your "FRESH WILL" components can be best enjoyed with those closest to you in your family. When that is not the case, another source of supportive, like-minded people can be found in your spiritual community, church, or synagogue. As you develop this sense of community in your life, you will both "give back" and "reach back." To give back is to teach someone else the lessons you've learned. To reach back is to talk to and encourage that person on a regular basis as they pursue their goals.

The output of your future reality facilitated through sustainability and community maximizes your impact by involving others to help you maintain, examine, appraise, and revise your plan to continually evolve and improve as you head toward your future reality. It brings to mind the ancient teaching from the Bible written by King Solomon, who Scripture called the wisest man to ever live. It says, "As iron sharpens iron, so one person sharpens another." (Proverbs 27:17)

> The output of your future reality facilitated through sustainability and community maximizes your impact.

That is so true! Together, we make each other better. We become receptive to new ideas, flexible, and teachable. We add value to one another. We invest of ourselves into the lives of others. We leave the world better than it was before.

That's leadership—and nothing is more important or inspiring.

By writing *Astronomical Leadership*, sharing the story of my personal journey, and imparting my Input / Process / Output approach to you, my heart is to inspire you to reach places you never thought you could, and to do it in a methodical way that will help you see and be amazed with your progress.

When I was growing up, I never thought I'd be where I am today. But by living out the principles I have presented here, I have achieved some incredible accomplishments more extraordinary than I could've ever anticipated. My current reality is truly amazing, and I am convinced my future reality is going to be even more remarkable. Just like I taught you, I've been there. I've called things that be not as though they were. I will see them come to pass. I am ready to up my game in a greater way, rewire my brain, and broaden my capacity and creativity. I am asking God to enable me to be able to do it in a way that is going to be astounding for His glory!

As a leader, and especially as a church pastor, I've observed that so many people don't see themselves as capable of becoming great, much less extraordinary. We settle for being average. We think we are fine just the way we are. But I believe we are created to succeed. To excel. To *be* extraordinary. I declare as true the words of Jesus Christ when He said of all of us, "I have come that they may have life, and have it to the full." (John 10:10) Other Bible translations render this as "life more abundantly." I love that! Yet there are so many people who never walk into the full measure of what their abundant life can be. We allow the past—mistakes we have made, or things that have been done to us—to create negative thinking that literally arrests us, keeping us imprisoned to it instead of breaking free from it.

I could've allowed my profound lack of self-confidence, and the words of others telling me what I couldn't do, to incarcerate me. I could've allowed my disappointment after the Columbia disaster to cripple me. But I didn't. Through all stages of my life, I worked hard. I learned. I grew. I dealt with my traumas through prayer and application of God's Word, and know you can, too. I overcame—and in the process I became all that I was created to be.

I didn't allow anyone else to write the script of my life for me. I wrote my own script, and through my approach that's exactly what you'll do. You'll participate in writing your own script. From positive planning to positive community to positive affirmations, you'll do it, and the sky is the limit. Actually, the sky is not the limit. You will reach further. You will go to the Moon and beyond!

My passion—and an integral part of my abundant life, my ongoing future reality—is to help you *be amazed at who you are* and discover your astronomical leadership!

You are ready. Together, let's get started.

Made in the USA
Middletown, DE
26 January 2019